The Public Sector

The Public Sector

Managing the unmanageable

Alexander Stevenson

KoganPage

LONDON PHILADELPHIA NEW DELHI

First published in Great Britain and the United States in 2013 by Kogan Page Limited

120 Pentonville Road	1518 Walnut Street, Suite 1100	4737/23 Ansari Road
London N1 9JN	Philadelphia PA 19102	Daryaganj
United Kingdom	USA	New Delhi 110002
www.koganpage.com		India

© Alexander Stevenson 2013

The right of Alexander Stevenson to be identified as the author of this work has been asserted by him in accordance with the Copyright, Designs and Patents Act 1988.

ISBN   978 0 7494 6777 7
E-ISBN   978 0 7494 6778 4

British Library Cataloguing-in-Publication Data

A CIP record for this book is available from the British Library.

Library of Congress Cataloging-in-Publication Data

Stevenson, Alexander.
    The public sector : managing the unmanageable / Alexander Stevenson.
      pages ; cm
    Summary: "The Public Sector: Managing the Unmanageable offers practical advice to public sector managers on how to develop techniques to deal with the challenges they face, particularly in the areas of accountability, setting targets, risk management/encouraging innovation, managing people, decision making and working with politicians. Based on original interviews with politicians and senior public sector managers, including the last four cabinet secretaries, it is full of anecdotes, actionable lessons and insights. Each chapter takes a specific aspect of management and starts by explaining why it is different in the public sector, then sets out ways for public sector managers to handle those differences and ends with an executive summary and a checklist to prompt managers to think about how they might change what they currently do" – Provided by publisher.
    ISBN 978-0-7494-6777-7 (pbk.) – ISBN 978-0-7494-6778-4   1. Public administration–Management.   2. Administrative agencies–Management.   3. Organizational effectiveness.   4. Organizational change.   5. Government productivity.   6. Political planning.   I. Title.
    JF1351.S83 2013b
    352.6'30973–dc23   2013006913

Typeset by Graphicraft Limited, Hong Kong
Printed and bound in India by Replika Press Pvt Ltd

CONTENTS

FOREWORD

Why does this book come at such an important time? Partly because public service management is a largely ignored subject, which is a spectacular oversight given the number of people employed in the public sector and its relevance to all our lives. It is patently obvious that managing the delivery of public services is not the same as bringing privately produced goods and services to market. There are different forces at work – public accountability is not the same as the bottom line – and a whole different set of disciplines and relationships operating. These need to be understood and improved if the public is to be served better.

But this book is also timely because, as a result of the 2007–08 financial crisis and the debt turnaround that government, banks and households will still be undergoing for years to come, the whole of the public sector is under pressure to change, becoming more efficient and offering more value for money than ever before. Indeed, as a result of the largest real-terms fall from peak to trough in public spending, a deeper recalibration of the state is likely to come about in the coming decade no matter which party or parties are in power. There will be a demand for equitable as well as efficient outcomes. Further moves away from monopoly providers are inevitable as the resources and skills of the private and third sectors are used more. How this greater competition in supply will be managed in combination with 'democratic' supervision will be an even bigger challenge than now. The public's quality of life and economic living standards are directly at stake. The careers of national and local politicians will be on the line. This will be the consequence of a trend rate of growth in the coming decade which if it is just 1 per cent below that of the decade prior to the financial crisis is likely to cost Europe €23 trillion in forgone economic capacity. The public sector will not escape the impact of this loss.

To be successful in navigating their way through this minefield, politicians and public service executives are going to have to be better than mere axe-wielders and spending-cutters – they will need to rethink, not just top-slice. And throughout, the public's needs and demands during these difficult economic times are going to grow as their demands for protection by the state mount. If ministers and local mayors and councillors are going to succeed in taking the necessary decisions (and stand a chance of being re-elected afterwards), they are going to require skill, inventiveness and ingenuity as they try to offer confidence and reassurance as well as change to an anxious public. And they cannot deliver this outcome alone. The whole of the public sector – management and workforce as well as their political masters – will have to understand the need for reform and, as a team, think through the recalibration of the state and its services that this implies.

This is why I think this book stands out and is so welcome. It is not a do-it-yourself guide to demolishing the public sector, quite the opposite. It addresses the ethos, goals and disciplines of public service and will help to create the means of refashioning and strengthening them. This is an intensely people-focused process. Running the public sector is about managing relationships – with the public, with the workforce, between managers and with politicians. If you do not persuade, inspire and offer adequate leadership, you will assuredly fail. If the process does not provide strong public accountability, it will be rejected. And if politicians find themselves unable to cope with the inevitable attack and occasional ridicule, they will become unbearable partners in the process.

In Britain, we have had two successive governments committed to public sector reform. Neither have got it completely right, the first because divisions at the top of the government ultimately led to the dilution and blunting of reform, and the second because neither goals nor means were clarified at the outset and necessary public support was not won over. The current generation now faces even greater challenges and complexity. They have to be even better at what the public sector has not always been good at in the past – listening to others, sharing knowledge and spreading and applying good practice.

When people ask me what I valued about being in government I honestly say trying to improve people's lives as a result of my actions. Of course, these outcomes were often intangible and distant but the process of interacting with my officials and public service managers has given me the greatest enjoyment in my life to date. I liked taking their analysis and advice and they in turn, I think, liked receiving firm, clear decisions from me. Occasionally I felt dissatisfied by the quality of advice I was receiving but I still had to take ultimate responsibility. In all circumstances I thought it was right to stand by my officials. Only once, soon after I had become a commissioner in Brussels, did I discover what it was really like to be at odds with your officials. Millions of items of clothing were growing into embarrassing textile mountains in ports around Europe as the volume of Chinese imports became the subject of deep contention between me and my leading trade official. The crisis passed and so did the official.

It is not fashionable to express respect for those who work in the public sector. The press and public alike love to pounce on failure. Sometimes, criticism is deserved. But there is no gain in demolishing the self-esteem of others or discouraging further the recruitment of bright, well-motivated young people who are often put off entering the public service not just by the frequently miserable earnings but by the prospect of being denigrated while undertaking thankless tasks in the public interest.

In Cabinet once I remember it being proposed that civil servants should have their pay cut to set a good example to everyone else. Why, I thought (and said), should such people be attacked just because they cannot fight back against political gimmickry? That is the price public servants pay for always being behind the scenes and unable to stand up for themselves. That is why they should be incentivized more, not less, in the positions they hold. Otherwise, how will we attract the best people to do and remain in their jobs? I am not saying civil servants are always in the right, of course not. I remember Tony Blair correctly insisting on the early retirement of one centrally placed senior official because this mandarin had become a permanent roadblock to reform in Whitehall. But if we want to encourage, as we should, boldness and risk taking in the public sector, we have to recruit the best and offer them proper recognition and rewards for the work they do.

The practicality of this book is its greatest value, including its advice about handling politicians. *Yes Minister* and *The Thick of It* are useful companion guides but I would defy anyone to identify better advice than that attributed in this book to Sir Hayden Philips when he describes the relationship thus: 'It's like an arranged marriage – you need to work hard and not be too judgemental on either side.'

Sir Humphrey could not have put it better. As for the rest of the book, it carves out a future path for the public sector which in many respects Sir Humphrey would not recognize or, I suspect, much sympathize with. And therein lie its immense interest and readability.

Lord Mandelson

Lord Mandelson served in the British Cabinet as the Secretary of State for Northern Ireland and the Secretary of State for Business Innovation and Skills. He was also the European Commissioner for Trade.

ACKNOWLEDGEMENTS

I relied on the generosity of a number of people both for the content of this book and for the encouragement and support I needed to write it.

First of all, I am extremely grateful to the interviewees for their time. Without their willingness to share their experiences so openly there would not be much of a book.

Secondly, I owe a debt of thanks to a long list of people whose brains I shamelessly picked at various points. In particular I'd like to thank: Ben Crewe, Ben Rowland, Chris Pearson, Ethan Kline, Geoff Mulgan, Grace Cassy, Helen Millichap, Henry Peterson, Hulya Mustafa, Janet Hughes, Marcial Boo, Michael Lea, Peter Taylor, Sarah Kline, Simon Tucker, Stephen Bampfylde, Vernon Bogdanor and Victoria Keilthy.

Special thanks are due to my old friend Nicholas Boys Smith. He gave me many of his precious family Sunday evenings, some spine-stiffening deadlines, bucketfuls of punchy insight and encouragement, and several delicious curries. Both the book and the experience of writing it were improved immeasurably by his involvement.

Finally, I would also like to thank Julia Swales, my patient editor at Kogan Page, for nurturing me through the process of writing this book so supportively and thoughtfully. I felt very lucky to have had her and Kogan Page on my side.

Given how many people have helped with this book, it is more than usually important to be clear that any remaining errors in judgement or fact are, of course, entirely mine.

ABOUT THE AUTHOR

Alexander Stevenson has worked as a private sector manager, as a successful entrepreneur and as an adviser to senior public sector managers. Having worked at the Financial Times Group, he set up RSe Consulting in 1999 with Ben Rowland. RSe provided management consultancy services to more than 150 public sector organizations and was bought by Tribal Group in 2008. Alexander currently has a variety of non-executive roles in the private and public sectors, including being a trustee of the Young Foundation and Fight for Peace UK.

Introduction – managing the unmanageable

This book is written primarily for public sector managers and those who work in some capacity with the public sector. As such, it is a rare breed. Although there are plenty of academic studies about the public sector, there are very few practical management books. By contrast, bookshop shelves heave with tomes devoted to every conceivable aspect of management in the private sector.

This is very odd. For a start, managing in the public sector is endlessly fascinating, far more so in most respects than managing in the private sector. There is much to write about and much to discuss.

Secondly, public sector management is hugely important. The public sector employs nigh on 20 per cent of the UK workforce and influences many of the things that matter most in our lives – our security, our environment and our health to name a few. If it is well managed we all benefit; if it is poorly managed we all suffer.

Finally, managing in the public sector is a distinct discipline and deserves to be treated distinctly. Of course, it shares features with private sector management. And of course, in some areas, public sector managers can learn from the practices of their private sector counterparts. But, in the main, public sector managers operate under specific constraints which make the processes of management very different and usually more difficult.

*

Like many practical management books it has a dramatic subtitle: *Managing the unmanageable*. This is designed to capture not just your attention but also the two major themes: first, that public sector managers face significant challenges; second, that there are ways of overcoming these challenges.

For public sector managers therefore, I hope it will prove both practically helpful and intellectually stimulating. For interested readers who do not work in the public sector I hope it will likewise be useful and stimulating and perhaps also offer a different perspective on the realities of managing in the public sector.

*

The drive for this book has come from my personal experiences with the public sector. In my mid-20s I set up, with a friend, a business which provided consultancy mainly to local authorities. This allowed me to learn about public sector management by observing at close quarters the practices of good (and occasionally bad) managers. It has also meant that I have become increasingly intolerant of the stereotype of the hapless, lazy, obstructive or even greedy public sector manager. Without looking too hard you can find people pro-pounding some form of this stereotype in the media, in many areas of the private sector and sometimes even self-deprecatingly within the public sector itself. This stereotype is not just plain wrong but also potentially damaging, not least to our ability to attract and retain the excellent public sector managers we all need.

The content therefore draws on these experiences and also on more than 60 interviews with public sector managers and politicians. Almost every area of the public sector is represented in these inter-views, but that is more through luck than design. The main con-sideration was to interview people whom I admired and who had interesting things to say about management. The majority of the interviewees have held, or do hold, very senior jobs in the public sector, but I also interviewed a number of middle managers to get a more grounded and (for most of us) familiar perspective.

Some consequences arise from using a wide range of interviews in a book. The main one is that with any luck it is accessible and read-able because it is full of real-life insight and anecdote. Another con-sequence is that in some areas no one point of view emerges. This is entirely appropriate. If there is a key lesson to take from what follows, it is that there is no single formula for managing successfully in the public sector. Rudy Giuliani was a ferocious centralizer when he was Mayor of New York. Michael Bloomberg, as you shall read, believes fervently in delegation. Both have been hugely successful. Different techniques will suit different people at different times, depending on the job, the circumstances, the people you have around you and indeed your own predisposition.

Although it is hard to summarize a book which contains so many individual insights and anecdotes, it is possible to extract some key points:

- Two factors above all else make life different for managers in the public sector – the lack of a single simple success measure and the need for democratic accountability. Both factors are largely unavoidable and both factors hugely complicate the processes of management, whether you are setting a strategy or targets, conducting an appraisal or managing risk.

- Four pieces of advice for dealing with these challenges stand out by virtue of the frequency with which they come up in the book and by the broad applications that they have. I return to them at greater length in the conclusion but in short they are:

  - Fully exploit the limitless comparative data. Almost every aspect of management can be made easier by having timely and accurate information about your peers – and as a public sector manager you have the privilege of access to this information without the barriers of competition to prevent you from getting it. Make the most of this managerial windfall.

  - Link people vividly to the ultimate impact of what they do. Some frontline workers, for example doctors, have an immediate connection with the people they are helping. But in many areas the link may be less obvious. Finding ways to make this link more vivid is useful in two ways: first of all, it provides first-hand information to help people do a better job; secondly, it should be inspiring and enthusing given that the ultimate goal of most public sector jobs is the inspirational one of improving the lives of others.

   – Focus on gathering soft feedback on the soft stuff. Many
     aspects of the work that public sector managers do cannot
     be held to account just by using numerical measures. Instead
     of spending time developing more complex levels of
     numerical reporting, public sector managers should think
     hard about ways of getting better feedback on the softer
     aspects of what they do.

   – Be proactive! As obvious as this may sound, the good
     managers that I know exhibit a restless energy and creativity
     which are focused on getting things done. They have been
     adept at resisting the (often legitimate) ways to procrastinate
     that the public sector can offer and ruthlessly efficient at
     navigating the necessary red tape.

● Finally, it is striking that two of the four pieces of advice – the
  limitless comparative data and linking people to their inspiring
  impact – are areas in which public sector managers have some
  practical advantages over their private sector counterparts.
  Both in exploiting these advantages and dealing with the
  unique challenges they face, public sector mangers should be
  consciously carving out their own management techniques
  rather than looking to the private sector.

How to use the book

Public sector management is a very broad topic. As a result this book
covers a wide range of experiences and subjects which will have vary-
ing levels of relevance depending on your own background. It may be
helpful, therefore, to imagine it as your personal sushi conveyor belt.
All sorts of delicacies will pass in front of your eyes. Some dishes you
will leave alone because you have had them before or because they do
not suit your tastes, others you will pick off and tuck away.

To help you do this, the book has a clear structure with plenty of
signposts. There are nine chapters and a conclusion. Chapter 1 sets
out the characteristics which make public sector management so
different and challenging.

Chapters 2 to 7 are the core of the book and cover the following management themes: accountability, target setting, managing risk/promoting innovation, managing people, managing politicians, decision making. Each chapter begins by exploring why these management areas are different in the public sector before offering advice on how to approach them. At the end of each chapter there is an executive summary and a checklist of questions.

Chapters 8 and 9 are more discursive. Chapter 8 suggests areas in which private sector managers can learn from their public sector counterparts. Chapter 9 assesses the status and significance of public sector managers and asks how we can continue to attract and retain the managers we need.

At the end of the book there is a conclusion, a list of the key insights and an index.

There are also biographies of all the people I have interviewed, which avoids me introducing them endlessly in the text. However, I have anonymized the majority of quotes from the middle managers because many felt sensitive making attributed comments about organizations for which they currently work.

Finally, I am painfully aware that it is a slightly absurd conceit to write about the public sector as if it is one entity. The public sector incorporates a huge variety of organizations, services and structures, many of which have very little in common. The same could be said of considering public sector managers as one group. Nonetheless, these are conceits that I have adopted in order to keep the book readable and ones which I hope you will tolerate.

The challenges of managing in the public sector

01

In 2005, Gill Rider was appointed Director of Leadership and People Strategy, the most senior Human Resources position in Whitehall. For the previous 27 years she had been working for Accenture where she became Global Chief Leadership Officer and a member of the executive committee. She says that in the first six months in her new role she felt as if she was swimming in treacle. 'At Accenture I was used to setting a policy one week and seeing it put in place all over the world the next. In government things moved much more slowly – it was a bit of a shock.'

But this was not due to the inherent inefficiency and incompetence of the public sector or the dead hand of government. For Rider her experience reflected the fact that managing in the public sector is more challenging. 'It is so much easier being a leader in the private sector – you have clarity of focus, a bottom line, a clear hierarchy. In the public sector it is just much harder.'

So what is it about the public sector that makes it so hard?

Two factors stand out – the lack of a single simple success measure and the need for democratic accountability. Both are inevitable in the public sector and both complicate the processes of management.

No single simple success measure

'There is a whole range of factors that are built into the way we run the company', says Michael Heseltine of his Haymarket Media

Group. 'These are what you might call the softer options; there's the human relations side of things and the environmental impact and the quality of dialogue with our staff and the quality of the products themselves. But at the end of the day the motive is to make a profit, the bottom line is survival. In the public sector it's infinitely more complex.'

In the private sector, success depends on the ability of an organization to create a profit, or in some cases, the promise of creating a profit. Not only does this simple measure allow anyone to assess easily the success of an individual organization – is it profitable or not – it also allows anyone to compare success between private sector organizations.

There is no such success criterion for the public sector. Instead, public sector managers (and politicians) juggle a number of often competing demands. This is true at a national level. Would you like Britain to concentrate on being wealthy? Equal? Powerful? Peaceful? Safe? Liberal? Healthy? Culturally rich? Fun? Probably all these things and more.

It is also true in most areas of public service. Helen Carter, a prison governor, gives a vivid insight into the different outcomes she juggles: 'I am often not sure what the public want the role of prison to be. Do people want prisons to be a place where people go as punishment? Do they want them to be a place that takes dangerous people off the street and confines them? Do they want them to be a place that fixes people and then sends them out never to offend again?' The answer is that different people and different politicians want different things at different times. It is Carter's job to interpret these aims and develop plans to deliver them.

It is not just the variety of success criteria that makes life challenging, but in some areas it is the difficulty of measuring them. There is no straightforward way of measuring the quality of a planning decision, for example. Nor is it easy to measure the impact that good (and bad) teachers have in a way which excludes the variables of language, environment and parental support.

And even when it is possible to measure things, the numbers are often only approximate measures of management success. One of the great apparent successes of Labour's time in government was the fall in NHS waiting lists. And yet arguably the main reason they fell was because the government decided to inject huge amounts of money and make it a political priority. The quality of the management, while important, was probably not the determining factor. Is this, therefore, a success? Or could the money have been better spent elsewhere?

This lack of a single success measure is the most significant difference between private and public sector management. It makes the task of managing exponentially harder in almost every key respect. It is harder to develop a strategy because you have to start by working out what outcomes you are trying to achieve. It is harder to assess the performance of your organization and the people within it without the benefit of straightforward measures. And, of course, without such clear assessments it can be harder to motivate people and make them feel accountable.

Fundamentally, almost every decision – strategic, operational, personal – is more difficult to make because the public sector manager does not have the luxurious simplicity of being able to ask 'Will this help us – or has this helped us – be more profitable?'

Democratic accountability

The second necessary spanner in the works is democratic accountability. Consider the differences for any business if overnight it became a democratically accountable organization. The life of senior managers would suddenly become a lot more complicated. For a start, they would have to put up with a 'shadow' opposition board who would seek to undermine their authority by criticizing them at every turn. Sometimes the shadow opposition would do it fairly, sometimes unfairly, but it would always be done as loudly and publicly as possible. In addition, all their decisions, expenses, salaries and performance data would be open to public and media scrutiny – and in all probability the negatives would get more coverage than the positives. And they would spend considerably more time communicating and thinking about communicating.

Michael Bloomberg is well qualified to comment on the differences. Having set up the global media company that bears his name, he has gone on to become Mayor of New York City and so has in-depth experience of working in both sectors. 'In business you do things out of the scrutiny of the public', he says. 'Sometimes you don't even have to tell your own employees. In government, because of laws that require disclosure and just the general ways governments work, the first thing you think about is how to communicate what you're doing and what the press will say. And it makes it really hard to experiment. If you try something new and it doesn't work, the word "*failure*" is the headline.'

'There are lots of "noises off"', says Charles Farr, the Director of the Office for Security and Counter-Terrorism. 'You operate under enormous public scrutiny. And it's not just the media, it's the oversight authorities. We appear before the Joint Committee on Human Rights, the Home Affairs Select Committee, the Intelligence and Security Committee and of course MPs.'

Michael Bichard recalls appearing in front of the Public Accounts Committee when he ran the Benefits Agency to answer questions about the Social Fund. This was a relatively small fund by central government standards – about £60m – designed as a benefit of last resort to provide people with basic items such as beds or gas cookers. It was also a nightmare to manage because it was hard to prove whether people deserved the benefit or to predict what the demand for these benefits would be like. 'But you had to bring that 60 million quid in on target at the end of the year. And if you got close to over-spending you were profligate and if you were under-spending then you weren't making use of the budget. I also remember being flagellated for not recovering more than 99 per cent of some budget or other. Most private sector companies would be absolutely delighted if 99 per cent of their invoices were actually paid and they were only chasing less than 1 per cent debt. But that's not good enough for the Public Accounts Committee.'

Of course, budgets are scrutinized and challenged in the private sector. But three factors make this sort of accountability arguably more challenging in the public sector. First of all, these conversations can take place in public or else details of the conversations may be made public if requested. Secondly, they might be led by politicians who have little experience of management or else are wilfully creating mischief. Thirdly, they may be reported by media outlets who may have even less understanding of management and potentially greater incentive to exaggerate and distort.

Thanks to social media this pressure is increasing as it becomes easier to share information quickly and often anonymously with a targeted audience. 'Sometimes I think the job is almost undoable', says Nick Walkley, who is now the Chief Executive of Haringey Council.[1] 'There is now nothing that I do internally that I don't consider public because so much is leaked.'

This public accountability does not just affect senior managers. It increases levels of bureaucracy throughout public sector organizations. In maths exam parlance, the public sector constantly needs to 'show workings' in order to justify its actions.[2] Meetings are minuted, predetermined processes are carefully followed and recorded, and decisions are not taken until every conceivably interested party has been consulted. Crucially, it can also inhibit public sector managers from taking risks. The upsides that private sector managers get from taking successful risks – recognition and money – are not large enough for public sector managers when weighed against the downsides of getting it wrong.

For managers in the public sector, therefore, democratic accountability can make it harder to do things quickly and less attractive to take risks.

Pressure?

In addition to these two factors, public sector managers can also experience enormous pressure. Of course, it is tempting to suggest that private sector managers face greater pressure. There is pressure to deliver sales, make profits, respond to competitors – with the looming pressure of keeping the business alive.

There is some truth in this, particularly for small businesses where the threat of going out of business can feel very immediate. I very much remember this pressure when managing my own small business where my business partner and I faced the relentless challenge of winning enough work to pay our 25 employees.

But while the public sector does not have the pressure of having to stay in business (unless bankrupt or being invaded), it has other pressures which can be just as difficult to manage. The first is the nature of the decisions being taken. Heather Rabbatts has worked in both the public sector and the private sector. Very little in the private sector, she says, can compete with the pressures that the public sector can throw at you. She describes one such example when, as Chief Executive of the London Borough of Lambeth, she was informed by a social worker that a potentially extremely violent man had been released from a mental institution. 'They'd rehoused him in Brixton where at the time you'd get a semi-automatic gun more easily than you'd get a McDonald's. So I had a frantic 24 hours to persuade people that this was not the right strategy and that he should be moved somewhere else, which thankfully he was. But those are the moments when you think "Oh my God, is somebody going to die on my watch?"'

'It is about being able to react in a level-headed way under the pressure of time', says Geoffrey Dear, the former Chief Constable of West Midlands Police. 'In business this rarely happens. You normally have enough time to react. The decisions are about sales, and profit and loss accounts and cash flows and can or can't we get the material in time and what are the competition doing.'

Of course, not every decision taken by a public sector manager will be quite as dramatic as those described by Rabbatts and Dear. But because the public sector is involved in so many areas which can have a significant impact on the quality of people's lives – whether it is education, social care, health care, transport, planning – the pressure to get these decisions right can be enormous.

Even in the area of revenue generation, public sector managers face pressures, albeit very different from those in the private sector. As a senior public manager you are often negotiating to secure your budget. You can be vulnerable to the whims of politicians who might decide to reorganize your department or slash your budget either for political or economic reasons for which you have no responsibility. And you will have few, if any, revenue-raising powers whatsoever – you certainly will not be able to set taxes and it is unlikely that you will be allowed to 'sell' products. In other words, you have very little control over how much money you receive. This might provide a comfort blanket for poor public sector managers. For the good ones it is incredibly frustrating – you have far less control over your destiny than you would like.

Compare the pressures of running Sky and the BBC. They are both high-wire acts. The chief executive at Sky faces daily judgement based on how much revenue he is generating from subscribers and advertisers as well as the Sky share price. And at regular intervals he has to explain himself to analysts in the City, not to mention his shareholders.

The Director General at the BBC has the daily judgement of viewing and listening figures. But this is not a simple accountability. He has to ensure not only that these figures are large, but also that they represent every demographic – he cannot choose his customers. He also has to report back to changeable and changing politicians and negotiate how much money his organization will get. And he does so while living with the constant albeit vague threat that the BBC, or at least large parts of it, may be privatized. In addition to this, every day there will be articles holding the BBC – and often the Director General personally – to account. These will cover a whole range of subjects such as bias in news coverage, the level of support the BBC provides for creative industries in the UK, the way that they distort the commercial market and, of course, how much they spend on salaries, programmes and biscuits.

This comparison applies generally. Like the Sky chief executive, most private sector managers need to produce profits and are accountable to shareholders. Like the Director General of the BBC, most public sector managers will face a complex matrix of key performance indicators, direct accountability to politicians and indirect accountability to the public via a mercurial media. There are pressures in both jobs but they appear in different forms.

The picture is also mixed when assessing who has the greater chance of holding on to their job. The average tenure of a FTSE 100 chief executive is almost six years. The average tenure of a local authority chief executive is between four and five. For NHS acute trust executives it is less than two and a half years.[3] Indeed, two of the last three Director Generals of the BBC – George Entwhistle and

Greg Dyke – have been forced to leave the role very publicly. I am not aware of any Sky chief executive ever being sacked. Either it has never happened, or if it has the sacking has taken place out of the public eye.

In summary: no single measure of success, democratic accountability, and a complex matrix of pressures. These are the constraints under which public sector managers operate. The next six chapters set out ways to deal with them.

Notes

1 When I interviewed Nick Walkley he was Chief Executive of the London Borough of Barnet, so unless otherwise stated his comments apply to his experiences there.

2 Academic analysis of the differences between public and private is consistent on this point more than any other – there is more red tape in the public sector. Chapter one of Christopher Pollitt's *The Essential Public Manager* (Open University Press/McGraw-Hill, Maidenhead, 2003) gives an excellent summary of the available literature and two particularly interesting papers are: G A Boyne, Public and private sector management: what's the difference? (*Journal of Management Studies*, 39 (1), 2002, 97–122) and H G Rainey and B Bozeman, Comparing public and private organizations: empirical research and the power of the a priori (*Journal of Public Administration Research and Theory*, 10(2), 2000, 447–69).

3 Will Hutton, Final Report of his Independent Review into Fair Pay in the Public Sector (HM Treasury, London, March 2011), 1.23.

Managing accountability

02

"If we don't have any terrorist attacks for a year, how do I know whether we've got lucky or whether we've been brilliant? **MAYOR MICHAEL BLOOMBERG, NEW YORK CITY**

This chapter concentrates on how to achieve better managerial (as opposed to political) accountability. The questions it deals with are:

- How do you ensure that the people working for you feel accountable for what they are doing?
- How do you achieve this when:
  - it is hard to measure the success of what they do;
  - it is hard to untangle their direct contribution to your goals from the contributions of others;
  - the impact of what they do may not be felt for many years to come;
  - their success or failure depends on the performance of partners or else on external factors beyond their control?

Introduction – the unaccountable lack of accountability

Shortly after the 1997 election, Jonathan Powell, the new Prime Minister's chief of staff, and his boss were briefed at 10 Downing

Street by officials from the Home Office. It was not good news. Crime was likely to rise as the success of the economy created greater divisions and more desirable goods for people to steal.

What, asked Jonathan Powell, would happen to crime if the economy started performing poorly? Ah, well, in that case, came the reply, crime would also go up as increasingly desperate people would resort to increasingly desperate measures to support their families. So, Powell concluded, no matter what happened, crime would rise and there was nothing that could be done about it.

This episode comfortably fits the stereotype of a public sector which is not accountable for what it does. This is the stereotype of a public sector in which public servants have jobs for life and fiddle around with bureaucratic processes which protect their backs while having little direct impact on the public.

It is the stereotype captured in General Sir Walter Walker's aphorism from the 1970s when he said: 'Britain has invented a new missile. It's called a civil servant – it doesn't work and it can't be fired.' And it is the stereotype that remains a mainstay of much of the political comment that we currently read. 'If a private company is found to be catastrophically incompetent by producing a lousy product, it goes bust', writes Melanie Phillips in one such article in the *Daily Mail*. 'But when the public sector is so incompetent... it treats this as a signal for paying itself even greater sums of public money.'[1]

There is much anecdotal evidence to support this stereotype. 'There are very few people that get sacked in the way that you would in the private sector,' says Peter Rogers, former Chief Executive of the City of Westminster and the London Development Agency, 'and there are very few people that are held to account for poor performance. And if you doubt that, have a look through any public sector body and find anybody that's really been dismissed for very poor performance – they are the exception rather than the rule.'

Hayden Phillips, a distinguished former Permanent Secretary, adds some weight to this view: 'The size of the civil service afforded me the luxury of being able to shuffle the pack and move people I found difficult or incompetent into roles that were either unimportant or else had no direct contact with me.'

One manager I spoke to was hired by a large central government department to set up a new communications team. The idea was that, like her, this team would be smart, ambitious and dynamic. It soon became clear to her that the department simply didn't have enough staff with the requisite skills. What is more, the department wanted her to hire from the internal pool of staff who were already without a position. This pool – which exists in a number of departments – is usually a mix of staff waiting for a short time for a new position, but can also be a way to deal with poor performers whose managers find it easier to move them sideways into the pool than to sack them or to invest time developing them. The staff are often on full pay but not working. For a year she struggled to train her inexperienced staff, some of whom had to be persuaded of the value of communications, and therefore their own role, before they could even start to make progress. She left the department within a year. The failure of the department to make people accountable for poor performance had the knock-on effect of blocking her ability to do a good job.

Good numerical evidence is harder to come by, but data produced by the Chartered Institute for Personnel Development (CIPD) lends some support to this picture. Using the numbers in its annual Resourcing and Talent Planning report we can surmise that on average, between 2007 and 2011, 6.7 per cent of the private sector workforce left their jobs involuntarily compared to 5.3 per cent of the public sector workforce.[2] However, it is of course hard among these aggregate figures to identify the people who were fired for performing poorly as opposed to being part of an organization experiencing general cuts.

In any case, the number of sackings is only one way of assessing levels of accountability, albeit the most visible. The proper test for good accountability should not be whether your staff feel nervous about losing their jobs but whether they feel as if what they do matters. 'People want to know two things,' says the Wandsworth Chief Executive Paul Martin, 'how their work fits into the organization as a whole and that their colleagues are interested in the quality of their work.' However, as the next section explains, it is not always easy to achieve such accountability in the public sector.

Why is it so hard to be accountable in the public sector?

There are several inherent features of the public sector which can make managerial accountability harder to achieve.

Political accountability can undermine the demand for managerial accountability

Living in a democracy means that in one sense we do have strong accountability for our public services. When things are going badly, politicians will be held to account via their constituents, via the media and ultimately via elections. If there is a major failing or crisis then ministers or MPs can be forced to resign, even over apparently operational issues for which they have little direct responsibility. For example, Charles Clarke lost his job as Home Secretary in 2006 shortly after it was revealed that the Home Office freed 1,023 foreign prisoners who should have been considered for deportation. This was clearly an operational issue. Data had been lost, processes had not been followed. And yet it was the politician who took the flak.

This political accountability undermines the strength of managerial accountability in a number of ways. First of all, managers who make mistakes may be less likely to lose their jobs. When the Home Office mistake was revealed, the pressure was piled onto Clarke rather than his officials and it was Clarke who lost his job. Thus in a very fundamental sense public sector managers are less accountable than their private sector counterparts.

Secondly, managers can get a new lease of life every time a different politician comes in. Indeed, it is part of their professional remit to be able immediately to dissociate themselves from the policies of the previous politician and devote themselves to the policies of the new one.

Finally, in theory managers are working in a structure where the politicians make the key policy decisions and their job is to deliver these policies. But in the simplifying and often simplistic glare of the public spotlight it is difficult to draw distinctions between failures of delivery and failures of policy. And so the default position can be that the politicians – and their policies – are responsible and therefore the public servants are not accountable. If the policies go well the politicians get the praise, and if they go badly they get the blame.

There can be a weak correlation between performance and results

In 2005, Gus O'Donnell set up a new initiative called capability reviews. These reviews provided a standardized way of measuring the performance of central government departments. What these capability reviews also highlighted is the separation between the quality of the work the departments do and the quality of the impact that they have.

In the first round of capability reviews, this was most starkly illustrated by the reports on the Home Office published in July 2006 and the Department for International Development (DfID) published in March 2007. The reviews assess each department in 10 categories which cover leadership, strategy and delivery. In each category the department is rated on a scale of one to five where one (Green) is 'strong' and five (Red) indicates 'serious concerns'. When you add up the 10 scores in their first capability reviews, DfID scores an impressive 25 whereas the Home Office scores a deeply unimpressive 37. The performance therefore of the Home Office was dire – or, as the review put it more diplomatically, 'urgent action is required to strengthen capability in key areas' – whereas the performance of DfID was excellent.

And yet when you look at the quality of the impact – what these departments actually achieved – the story is very different. The Home Office which John Reid had famously described only a few months before the capability review as being 'not fit for purpose' was producing great results. Crime rates were flattening, fear of crime was down, unfounded asylum claims were down and at last the numbers of asylum cases being cleared exceeded the number of new asylum claims entering the system. In fact, the Home Office was delivering on every single one of its Public Service Agreement targets.[3]

DfID's achievements appeared to be more modest. It was making 'significant progress'[4] against its targets. However, it was falling behind on 8 of its 31 sub-targets and the review reported coyly that progress towards the high-profile Millennium Development Goals remained 'most challenging'.[5] In other words, the department which was judged to be the worse performer was apparently producing much better results than the department which was judged to be the better.[6]

Of course, the correlation between the quality of an individual's performance and the results achieved is rarely perfect in either the public or the private sector so it can make sense to attempt to measure them separately. But because the outcomes are so often more complex and harder to measure in the public sector, there is the potential for people to feel less accountable for results. Moreover, the mechanisms for measuring the quality of performance are rarely as well funded or robust as the capability reviews. The upshot is that the incentives to perform well may be less, and mediocre performance may not be identified quickly.

Consider the number of different people involved in keeping New York City safe. At one level there are the strategic decisions made by the US President and the Mayor in areas like foreign policy, immigration, crime and education. Then there are the public officials implementing these decisions, for example the police officers, the embassy officials, the immigration teams. And then there are wider, less direct contributing factors such as the strength of the economy or the progress of science in developing new types of safety equipment or bombs, or even the tone of the media. It is hard enough to judge the impact that any one of these organizations has had, let alone the impact that any individual within them has had.

Or take the upbringing of a child. How is it possible to distinguish the influence of a social worker from that of a teacher or a parent, or for that matter the area in which the child lives? And on top of that, how can you quickly assess the success of interventions by a social worker which may not bear fruit for many years to come?

In each of these instances and many more, it is possible for an individual to perform excellently or poorly and have little discernible impact on outcomes.

It is sometimes hard to define what you do

Another challenge is defining what to be accountable for. When John Ransford became Chief Executive of Kirklees Metropolitan Council in 1987, one of his first 'getting to know you' meetings was with the chief executive of the local electricity board. 'Our purpose is to deliver electricity as cleanly, cheaply, safely and reliably as possible', he told Ransford. 'What is yours?' Ransford was stumped. What was the local authority's purpose? To improve people's lives? That was so general as to be meaningless. To make the area safer, greener and cleaner? Well, yes, but it was not as if he as chief executive of the local authority was able to control all these things or would even want to. And even these broad terms would not cover everything that the local authority was meant to do. No, there was just no straightforward way of summing up his organization's purpose and therefore no easy specific way to hold him to account.

Ransford's dilemma echoes the challenge Helen Carter described of trying to meet the multiple and often conflicting demands of being a prison governor. So many roles in the public sector have multiple goals, which means that accountability is far from straightforward.

But these multiple goals are not limited to senior posts. In 2010, Kevan Collins, the Chief Executive of Tower Hamlets, took part in the Channel 4 programme *Undercover Boss*. The premise of the programme is that the boss works on the frontline of their organization without revealing their true identity in order to understand their organization better. One of the jobs allocated to Collins was the delivery of meals on wheels. This was poignant because at the time he was considering outsourcing the service in order to realize some much-needed savings for the council. Even allowing for the romance of television the impact of delivering the service himself appeared to affect him greatly. He realized that to be more cost-effective the staff needed to spend less time with the housebound customers when delivering the meal. But he also realized that this time spent with people, some of whom would otherwise have very little human contact, was in many ways the most valuable part of the service, not just because it made them happier but also because often the meals on wheels staff would direct them to other services that they might need, potentially saving the council money in the long run. 'Going out with meals on wheels has been really good for me,' he concludes in the programme, 'because it reminds you that when you are looking for your efficiencies, there is a cost, a real cost.'

Collins' experience illustrates the management challenge that multiple goals can present. The staff delivering meals on wheels need to ensure that food is delivered on time, that it is fresh and hot, that they make the recipient feel valued and that, where appropriate, they identify other ways in which they might help. Of these, the main output that Collins was able to manage was the financial one – how much was the service costing and could it be delivered more quickly. He had no straightforward mechanism for recognizing or rewarding the efforts that people would make to deliver on the other goals because there was no easy way to capture what the service's purpose was.

It is difficult to observe directly what the public sector does and achieves

Ransford and Collins might have been comforted by reading James Q Wilson's excellent, if unalluringly titled, *Bureaucracy*. Wilson groups organizations according to whether their outputs and outcomes can be observed by managers. The easier it is to see what people do and what they achieve, the more accountable they will be.

At one extreme is an organization like the Inland Revenue (now HMRC) where it is easy to observe both the significant outputs (letters or audits by the tax inspectors) and the significant outcomes (how much tax is collected). Wilson calls this a production organization and these are the most straightforward types of organization to manage. Most private sector organizations would fall into this category – their output being a product and their desired outcome being profit.

An example at the other end of the spectrum might be social care, where it is impractical to observe the output (social workers with their clients) systematically and hard to determine the outcome (their clients leading happy and fulfilling lives). Wilson calls this a coping organization and these can be the hardest types of organizations to manage.[7]

Unfortunately for the public sector manager, very few public service agencies come under the production organization banner. For example, of more than 800 services provided by local authorities, fewer than 100 have easily observable outputs and outcomes – and typically these are the least important services such as registering births, deaths or pets.[8] For many public sector services there is no easy way for managers to observe both the outputs and outcomes of the services they are delivering, which adds to the challenge of being accountable.

How to create accountability

I made people accountable through blind terror... you pick up the phone and you say 'if you wish to be working here at the end of the week then you are going to do this'.

KEN LIVINGSTONE, FORMER MAYOR OF LONDON

Blind terror may work for some, but below are some alternative ways of enhancing accountability.

Compare yourselves with your peers

Knowing that your performance will be compared directly to that of your peers is a powerful motivator whether for organizations or individuals. In the private sector it seems easy to make these comparisons. At a corporate level, companies compare overall results and profits. And these items can often be compared at an individual level too. Job security, pay and status will depend on these results.

In the public sector it can appear to be harder to make such direct comparisons. Indeed, one of the justifications for bringing the private sector in to deliver public services is that because they are naturally comparing themselves so often with their rivals they will be more cost-effective and innovative.

And yet in many ways the opportunities for embedding these comparisons and driving efficiencies and innovation are much greater and more exciting for public sector managers. Most public sector organizations have very directly comparable peers – and there are no competitive pressures which prevent them from sharing the details of their performance with each other. Hospitals can share data with other hospitals just as police forces in one part of the country can do so with those in another part of the country, and it is even possible to draw sensible comparisons internationally too.

It is a fantastic resource to have – imagine how much O2 would pay to have ongoing access to information about all the internal workings and performance data of Vodafone. Imagine, too, how much time O2 would invest in making the most of this information. Instead, their detailed knowledge of each other is at best likely to be incomplete and at worst inaccurate.

And the public sector has another advantage. Not only can public sector bodies use this data to challenge their own performance, but where they spot their 'competitors' outperforming they can find out how they do it and legitimately steal their ideas. Comparing yourself with your peers will not just increase accountability, it will also increase performance.

Of course, these comparisons already happen to some extent in the public sector. There are benchmarking groups, mutual inspection re-gimes and national bodies which collect performance data centrally. But there is usually the potential to do more by collecting better data and spending more time understanding it. Do you and your team have regular and accurate performance data on your peers? Can you satisfactorily explain any discrepancies that exist?

'Comparing with other London boroughs is the best comparison I could have', says Robin Wales, the directly elected Mayor of Newham. 'I would like to know in real time every quarter where we sit in com-parison to other London authorities.' For Paul Martin the use of comparative data is key to the success of a manager: 'It is a sign of strength when managers proactively seek these sorts of comparisons to learn from and a sign of weakness when either they do not attempt it or else obfuscate the results by saying "It's impossible to compare us with so and so because we are so different."'

When used properly, comparison is powerful. Detective Inspector Helen Millichap works in Newham. She described to me the experience of attending a monthly meeting called Crime Fighters at the Metropolitan Police where representatives from all the London boroughs go to review their performance:

> A set of data is produced which records numbers around violence reduction, robbery reduction, burglary reduction and detection. It starts off at a general level with what the Met is doing well, what is medium and where there are problems. Then it really starts to bite when you get to comparisons between specific boroughs. The data starts to tell a story that may indicate weaknesses or vulnerabilities within the borough that you might not have noticed. So we're an outlier at the moment in Newham on theft. We think we can attribute this to a new shopping centre but nonetheless we will be under the spotlight and asked questions. There may be an explanation. But it may genuinely be a vulnerability and there may be actions required.
>
> They also circulate good practice from the Crime Fighters sessions. One of the recent bits came from a London borough which was putting direct surveillance in place on shops that were reselling stolen mobile phones. We did an operation like this here last week and had some success with it.

On the subject of mobile phone theft, Michael Barber, who set up the Prime Minister's Delivery Unit, recalls using international peer comparisons to challenge the police. 'When we started cutting crime in 2002, the first thing the police said was: "Well, if you give us more money we will flatten the rate of increase." And we said: "No, we don't want to slow the increase, we mean crime has got to go down. And we want it to go down fast." Their response was: "We won't be able to do that because there are more and more mobile phones. And they are half of all street robberies." I said: "There are more and more mobile phones in New York, but crime is falling. If that is happening there, why isn't it happening here?"'

Nick Walkley describes how comparative data helped him drive improvements as Chief Executive of Barnet Council:

> In this place everybody thought we had a good council tax service [as measured by the percentage of council tax collected]. Where we performed less well people would say 'We're not like X', or 'We're not

like Y.' But the moment Hackney overtook us there was this enormous incentive to figure out what was going on and there were just some really simple things we were getting wrong that managerially we could sort out. And that's a really powerful message.

The best example of this is actually the quality of street cleanliness across London, where that collective measuring has formed an incentive to learn from each other and drive standards up. And we know this from our own day-to-day walking-about experience. The gathering of the data, use of that data, has qualitatively changed the quality of people's lives.

This peer pressure can also come from within. 'Often nobody actually knows, other than the manager, whether that particular member of staff has succeeded or not', says Brian Dinsdale. 'I think that's wrong. I think that organizations ought to be very transparent about what is being expected of people. You can plaster the walls with statistics, have a monthly newsletter where achievements are highlighted, you can bring in annual awards for exceptional performance. There is a variety of ways of making achievements obvious to the organization, and making individuals in the organization proud of what they have achieved.'

But this internal transparency is not just there to celebrate good performance. Dinsdale continues:

Where parts of the organization haven't performed, you have to make everyone aware of it and how you are dealing with it and being supportive. What that also instils is a desire by the people in the organization to perform because they're aware that if they don't perform, then it's going to be known. In one authority where I was chief executive there was a very obvious breach in budgetary control in social services, which meant that the authority was going to start overspending considerably. That was made very clear, right throughout the council, along with the steps that were being taken to try to correct it because the result was that other services were being deprived of resources. So it's about highlighting issues, what effect they are going to have and what the management are doing constructively about it. I just think that being transparent is the right thing to do.

Get people as close as possible to the impact they are having

The trick is to make the accountability as personal as possible. This gets over the inevitably unquantifiable aspects.
HAYDEN PHILLIPS

As well as access to almost limitless comparative data, the public sector has another asset when it comes to enhancing accountability – the majority of the work the public sector does is ultimately for the benefit of other people, and for the people doing the work that should be very motivating. The managerial challenge is how to squeeze the most out of this natural advantage.

On 23 March 2012, the comedian John Bishop was taking part in the BBC's Sport Relief night. He had already raised millions of pounds by cycling, rowing and running over 295 miles from Paris to London in five days. His next task was to persuade the British public to donate even more money for Africa on the night. He talked about the challenges that some Africans face and the good work that Sport Relief does. He then went on to acknowledge how remote all this must seem to us as we sat watching our televisions in the UK. 'But,' he concluded, 'if someone said to you that someone on the other side of the road would die if you didn't give them five pounds, you would.'

In using this personal language, John Bishop was doing his best to make us feel accountable for a problem that was many thousands of miles away. He was appealing to our better nature and bringing the impact that we could have as close to us as he could. Public sector managers have it easier. Typically the impact of what they are doing is much closer to hand. At the same time they will often, like Sport Relief, have an inspiring cause to motivate people.

Getting close to this impact happens automatically in some jobs. Doctors are good examples of this. I spoke to one who has been working consistently more hours than he is paid for throughout his career. 'You just have to get the job done,' he reflects, 'because the consequences of not doing it are so obvious.' In terms of making him feel accountable, being face to face with his patients and their families is hard to beat.

This is harder to achieve in other areas of the public sector. Even jobs that are considered frontline do not necessarily bring staff into direct contact with the people who are benefiting. At one extreme frontline, the armed forces are face to face with the enemy often thousands of miles away from the people they are protecting and in a very alien environment. Perhaps this is why so much effort is put into reminding them of the support they have back home. We need to remind them what they are protecting and why they are doing the job that they do. At another extreme, traffic wardens will spend most of their time dealing with angry motorists rather than the local people whose parking spaces they are preserving. And of course there are whole sections of the public sector – not least the managers themselves – who rarely if ever come into contact with the people who are benefiting from their actions.

Michael Bichard describes how he thinks about this challenge and how he applied this thinking when he was Permanent Secretary at the Department of Education:

> The really effective public sector managers are the people who can connect their teams with outcomes and with outcomes on the ground. I always think it's a hugely undervalued skill of public sector leaders to connect their people with the reality of their impact. I always found it odd in the department [of Education] when I went there that initially I had to legitimize civil servants going out to schools because they hadn't done that. As they saw it, going to Croydon for a couple of hours to sit in on a class, which meant you had to spend an hour to get there and an hour to get back, was half a day out of the office. But when it did happen the impact on people could be absolutely electrifying. Sitting in on a literacy and numeracy class with a young teacher can be inspiring. It is partly about getting people to understand just how powerful they are, where so often we hear complaints about not having enough power. People, actually very young people, particularly in the civil service, have a lot of power and influence and that's something which is very exciting. I don't always see public sector leaders bringing that out.

Helen Carter described an episode illustrating how proximity to an issue brought about this level of personal accountability in a prison:

> When I was at my last prison there was an 82-year-old man who was due to be released. However, he was at the end of his sentence and so not on any form of reporting to probation. But the staff came to me and said 'We can't just release this guy. He can't look after himself.' He had been assessed for a residential care home, but they wouldn't take him because he was a high MAPPA [multi-agency public protection arrangement] risk which meant that he was a risk to other people even though he was quite elderly.
>
> So they won't take him in residential care. But we couldn't just let him go, we couldn't just put him in a taxi and send him to the train station saying there's your travel warrant. And staff stayed several hours beyond their shifts until they found him somewhere to go, as even though it was not our statutory responsibility it was the right thing to do. In situations like this you will always have the staff who go above and beyond and take things on as a real sense of 'This is my job and I will not let this person down.'

In this last example the accountability the prison officers feel is naturally towards the prisoner. They can immediately see how their actions affect the prisoner's well-being. But prison officers are also having a positive impact on two further groups of people: first of all, the victims of the crime for whom the prison provides some retribution, and secondly, the reformed prisoners who go on to lead fulfilling lives which contribute to society. If prison officers were to spend time with both these groups in addition to the existing prisoners then it would in all likelihood improve both their enthusiasm and their ability to do their job well. In particular, by spending time with reformed prisoners – instead of just welcoming back re-offenders – they would see the fruits of their labour and also learn what has worked so that they could transfer those lessons to their daily work.

By thinking where the ultimate impact of their work is felt and how to bring this vividly to life for their staff, managers can ensure that staff have a clearer sense of their accountability, are more inspired to do their job and do it more effectively.

Establish a narrative for your organization

I quoted Paul Martin earlier in this chapter saying that everyone should know how their work fits into the organization as a whole. This is the impact that a good narrative should have – it ensures that people feel as if what they do matters. In other words, they feel accountable.

Here is an example. A senior Oracle manager told me that Larry Ellison, the larger than life founder and Chief Executive of Oracle, has a straightforward but slightly menacing test. When he comes across an employee he hasn't met before, he says: 'If you don't sell, support or develop software then you'd better tell me very slowly and carefully what exactly it is you do for this business.' This mantra is indicative of a clear narrative. As an Oracle employee, you can easily assess how useful you are being to the organization.

Most public sector organizations require a more complex narrative than Oracle. But it is worth the effort. A clear narrative can be even more useful in the public sector than the private sector. It can transcend the complexities of the detail. Knowing as a health visitor, for example, that your primary aim – your narrative – is to give your elderly patients the best possible quality of life is a lot clearer than being judged according to a series of processes or targets. It makes it far easier to prioritize what should be done and should also lead to better outcomes for the patient.

Narratives in the public sector should also be inspiring. Speaking on the BBC business programme, *The Bottom Line*, in March 2011, the Britvic Chief Executive Paul Moody shared what he considered to be his most important business lesson: 'I think it's really important to deliver a clear and inspirational message about where the business is going.' It might be easy to deliver a clear message about where the business is going but coming up with an inspiring message for an organization whose main activity is to sell soft drinks is much more challenging. The public sector has the opposite challenge. The narrative should at the very least be inspirational – by and large, public sector bodies exist primarily to improve people's lives – but making it clear can be difficult. Occasionally, public sector strategies can sound drearily like their private sector counterparts. Instead, they should aim to be exciting narratives which exploit the fact that they are doing work of which people should be proud.

For James Purnell, another advantage of a strong narrative is that it enables you to ride out short-term crises. Most people will not remember the schools funding crisis in the spring of 2003. To remind you... at this time a change in the way that schools were funded meant that a significant number of schools ended up with less money than they should have done. Unsurprisingly, the head teachers involved kicked up a fuss, as did the opposition. But, says Purnell, 'the crisis was largely ignored because of the wider story about Blair's school reforms'. In other words, because the government's narrative around education was so strong (who can forget the mantra 'education, education, education'?), the funding 'crisis' was viewed as a small blip in a much larger, well-intentioned programme.

Narrative was also important to Helen Bailey when she became Chief Executive of the London Borough of Islington in 2002. Five months after her appointment the Audit Commission rated the performance of Islington 'poor' – the lowest mark it could award. The narrative that Bailey constructed together with the political leadership in response to this had two elements – first of all, she told the world that the council would be rated 'good' within four years, and secondly, they would do it together as one organization. 'I was determined we were not going to have the rest of the organization point their fingers at the bits that weren't doing so well as if it was nothing to do with them. And if there was a success – perhaps we won an award or someone said something good about us – everybody would celebrate. And if something went wrong everybody would say "What can we do to help?"'

Bailey backed this up in a number of ways both large and small. She branded everything she could with the Islington Council logo – and to ensure this happened properly she even walked around the borough noting down council vehicles that did not have the new logo on them and taking whatever opportunities she could to reinforce the message that they were one organization. 'I remember walking past one of our buildings which we branded Contact Islington and somebody who worked there said to me, "I really don't like that." And I said, "Why not?" "Because," he said, "I don't work for Contact

Islington, I work in the public health bit of environmental services." So I said to him, "Well, look, think about when you go to your local council where you live, do you always know which bit of service it is you're looking for? Or are you just wanting to contact your council?"'

She also embedded the practice of working across departments from her management team down. A month before any report went to the public executive to be scrutinized by the politicians, she would go through it at a joint board meeting with all her managers. This was partly good practice – a report from one department might have a previously unseen impact on another – but it was also about encouraging them to work together as a team. Islington achieved the 'good' rating within three years.

When Peter Rogers was the Chief Executive of the London Development Agency (LDA), he created a different kind of narrative. The LDA was responsible for developing and delivering an economic strategy for London until, like all other regional development agencies, it was closed by the Coalition Government in 2012. It reported directly to the mayor of London and had an annual budget of around £500m. Rogers became chief executive in 2008 following the election of Boris Johnson as mayor.

When he joined the LDA, Rogers immediately set about developing a narrative for it. 'The first thing I did was to ask the top 30 or 40 managers what the agency was about and the answer I got was not a very good one. There was no coherent view about what this organization did.' His response was to develop a three-pronged mantra of 'jobs, skills and growth'. Through systematically cascading this message throughout the organization this mantra has become the narrative of the organization 'so that everyone can repeat what we stand for'.

But sometimes a good narrative is hard to find. During the course of my working life, and the research for this book, I have come across any number of meaningless narratives. Typically these fall into two categories, the ridiculously broad or the absurdly obvious. The impact is the same. They do not help people work out what they should be doing. In turn, this can make it hard for people to feel accountable and harder still for managers to assess how good a job they are doing.

'There were plenty of corporate plans from the late 1990s and early 2000s that were effectively just a multicultural family on a roundabout', says Nick Walkley, 'because that was all they could agree on. But it has no bite, no meaning.' By contrast, the narrative Walkley developed at Barnet was about growth. 'Everyone should ask themselves, "What am I doing to sustain business in Barnet?" Because we need business to drag people along and to create revenues to deliver effective public services.'

But even so, he feels that narratives should be treated with caution. 'The golden thread is a convenient HR shorthand for the sophistication of good management. I actually think it is motherhood and apple pie dressed up as a coherent diagram to satisfy auditors. What you're really looking for are good people capable of expressing their contribution to making their service good in real terms and making a wider contribution. But that's a much more complicated message than "There's something at the top that everybody connects to."'

So what can we make of this? Sometimes there is a burning platform which creates the sort of narrative that Helen Bailey was able to articulate for Islington. At other times there is a big strategic – and often political – narrative such as the Labour Government's focus on education described by James Purnell. But more often than not, narratives are likely to be rather more functional and not, in my view, worth agonizing over. The key test for a narrative is the one articulated by Paul Martin, namely that people should be able to understand how their work supports the overall objectives of the organization. Photographs of roundabouts are unlikely to help.

When in doubt, devolve – but there is room for quite a lot of doubt

While most managers will agree on the need for some sort of narrative, the decision about how much to devolve in the cause of making people accountable is much more delicate. Devolve too much and you lose your ability to understand and influence what your team are doing; devolve too little and people will not take responsibility for their actions or feel accountable for them.

When he was Mayor of New York, Rudy Giuliani had a sign on his desk which read simply: 'I'm responsible.' This philosophy was the cornerstone from which he developed a command-and-control style of management. Every morning at 8 o'clock he held a meeting with his top 15 to 20 managers. 'The morning meeting was the core of my approach to managing', he writes. 'It served numerous purposes – decision making, communicating, even socializing – but most of all it kept me accountable. The morning meeting was where the chief executive was responsible and could hold everybody else responsible.'[9]

By contrast, his successor, Michael Bloomberg, has a more devolved approach to managing New York City which he sums up in a colourful analogy: 'My house doesn't belong to me or my girlfriend, it belongs to my housekeeper – she's the one who takes the key decisions about how it looks and when things get done and so she must feel ownership of it.' Thus at work Bloomberg will set a clear direction but then seek to give away as much responsibility as possible to his staff. He is clear about the difference between his approach and Giuliani's: 'My predecessor centralized everything so that he or someone in his office made every decision... but I don't happen to think that that is the right way to get on a track with the best people.'

The trouble – at least for somebody trying to learn lessons about management styles – is that both have worked. By almost any measure Giuliani and Bloomberg have been among the most popular and successful New York mayors of all time.

But it does neatly set up the dilemma for a public sector manager, indeed for any manager. On the one hand, setting targets and processes can enhance accountability by helping people understand clearly what they are responsible for. And it helps the manager keep on top of what is going on. On the other hand, devolving responsibility can deliver effective accountability because people will put more effort, pride and imagination into something that they feel they own.

In both the public and private sectors, managers may sometimes talk in terms of devolving responsibility but will end up putting in processes and targets. They will want to be Bloomberg but end up as Giuliani or a hybrid of the two.

You can see these different approaches at work in the way that people responded to the death of Baby Peter at the hands of his mother, her boyfriend and a lodger on 3 August 2007. During the course of his 17-month life, public agencies (mainly health and social services) had come into direct contact with Baby Peter and his mother more than 60 times. And yet they were not able to prevent his death.

The initial Serious Case Review produced by Hackney's Local Safeguarding Children Board identified significant failings. There were failings in process. Critical information about Baby Peter was not shared effectively between agencies and key individuals did not turn up to meetings. The upshot of these failings was to make it harder for the agencies involved to take well-informed decisions about Baby Peter.

And there were failings in the decisions made by individuals. Certain situations 'should have been responded to more authoritatively' or were 'accepted too readily'. It states that reasonable interpretation of the evidence 'should have guided the initial inter-agency response'. Perhaps the most poignant image is the visit by a social worker who found Baby Peter covered in chocolate – possibly to cover up bruises. The social worker did ask for this to be washed off but did not then take a look at Baby Peter once this had been done.

If you had been Ed Balls – Secretary of State for Children, Schools and Families at the time – what would your response have been? Would you have viewed this as an issue to be dealt with through introducing more stringent processes to ensure that data was shared effectively? Or would you have viewed this as an issue requiring a change in culture ensuring that frontline staff felt more emboldened to take responsibility and use their initiative?

Would you have been Giuliani or Bloomberg?

In the event, Ed Balls tried to do both but ended up on the centralizing Giuliani route. He emphasized the importance of changing the culture around children's social care so that people accepted more responsibility while at the same time he commissioned a review into the case from Lord Laming. This review ended up producing 58 recommendations, most of which he accepted. Among these recommendations were plans for new frameworks, new guidance and even a whole new central organization to deal with child protection.

For Ken Livingstone this was the wrong solution. There were already too many frameworks and processes, not too few: 'When management processes come in, individual accountability gets lost as people imagine that they are protected by those processes.' This is certainly a philosophy that a large number of managers would espouse. And yet there are some very rational reasons why Ed Balls did what he did.

First of all, it is much easier to identify and improve poor processes than it is to identify and improve a poor culture. Assessing the culture of a single organization, let alone a profession, is a tricky task, and changing it can be a long and inexact journey. Secondly, it is also much easier to satisfy the public demand that 'something must be done' by visibly changing processes rather than talking airily about culture change and responsibility. Finally – and perhaps a trifle cynically – it will take a long time to assess whether what Ed Balls did has worked, and even over time it will be hard to judge as circumstances (and governments) change. His reforms may be right. But it is impossible to say that they are.

So what conclusions should be drawn? Is it best to be command and control or to set a culture? Do you give yourself the comfort of process and knowing precisely what is going on, with the risk that you stifle the people working for you? Or do you create an environment in which people take more personal responsibility with the risk that mistakes are more likely to be made which will be blamed on you?

These types of decision are faced every day by managers at all levels of the public sector. There is a school of thought which says that the public sector needs command and control precisely because it is so hard to pin down and that without such an approach it risks becoming very woolly. And there is another school of thought, articulated by former Chancellor of the Exchequer Nigel Lawson, that 'the complexity of the public sector makes it folly to try and tie everything down. Instead you need to create a public sector ethos in which everyone does their best.'

On balance there is a case for saying that when in doubt managers should delegate. The main reason for saying this is that the natural instinct will be to do the opposite. The pressures of meeting targets, of having to follow set processes and of public scrutiny mean that often managers will be reluctant to let things too far out of their control and their staff therefore feel less personally accountable and responsible for what they do.

There is no panacea but instead a host of variables to consider, including:

1 **Your personal style and character.** It is hard to imagine Giuliani being comfortable without knowing precisely what was going on no matter how much he trusted and rated his staff. A culture with few measures and even fewer standardized processes in place would have ensured real tension. He would no doubt have been looking over people's shoulders at their performance and would have been frustrated. At the same time there is no point in having lots of targets/management information if you are not the type of person who will use it.

2 **The type of people working for you.** Although to some extent your staff need to adjust their styles to your way of working more than the other way round, at the same time, one of the skills of management is to develop a sense for what sort of management style most suits the people around you. Some will relish personal responsibility; others may feel uncomfortable without a clear structure.

3 **The significance of the service.** Some services are so significant – not least the protection of vulnerable children – that it is important for the senior manager to have a reasonable grasp of what is going on. In these areas, therefore, one would expect to see greater use of targets and tightly defined processes.

4 **The quality of data available.** Typically, if performance data is readily available and straightforward to analyse – for example punctuality of trains – it is easier for managers to devolve responsibility; if they are more ambiguous or simply harder to collect, managers are likely to be more reluctant to do so.

Does performance-related pay improve accountability?

In addition to all the strategic ways of achieving accountability mentioned above, the subject of performance-related pay came up time and again in the course of the interviews. However, there was no agreement about its effectiveness.

On one side Andrew Turnbull, the former Cabinet Secretary, articulates the case for performance-related pay: 'Bonuses help breed accountability, not for the amounts you pay out but for the process you have to go through of agreeing objectives, monitoring them and then reviewing them at the end of the year.' He is supported by a former Permanent Secretary at the Home Office, David Normington. He feels that awarding bonuses on a comparative basis (ie not everyone gets the top bonus) 'forces a set of discussions you might not otherwise have'.

Another former Cabinet Secretary, Richard Wilson, feels differently: 'There is a sense in which management accountability is more powerful if it's separated out from things like bonuses.' In other words, people will feel more motivated if they are seen to be doing a good job for the sake of it rather than for any extra money. He also thinks the amounts involved are a factor – 'The size of bonus that the public sector is able to pay out is usually so small that it is not going to be seen as a huge incentive.'

Brendan Barber, the General Secretary of the TUC, shares his misgivings on slightly different grounds. He worries that it is impossible to come up with a fair system for distributing bonuses and also that the very concept of individual bonuses undermines the teamwork which is so critical to good public sector service delivery – 'It's not always easy to disentangle which member of the team is most responsible for creating success or failure.'

Michael Bichard is a fan of performance-related pay provided it is used properly – and in his experience it often is not. 'If you're going to have a bonus and if it's going to be an incentive then it means that you're not always going to get it. In almost every job I've been in I have had crap thrown at me and had demoralized staff because I wouldn't accept that everyone should get 100 per cent bonuses. With bad managers a bonus just becomes a sweetie to hand out at the end of the year and I don't think it's defensible.'

Gill Rider has changed her mind about performance-related pay:

I used not to believe in performance-related pay because I thought people would just do the right thing regardless. But actually I think it is motivating to tie achievements to money even if the amounts are small.

It forces more honest conversations. Even if you have forced rankings or different bandings of performance, the conversations about where people are placed are likely to be more charged if money is involved. However, many of my colleagues disagree and I have yet to see any examples of this working well within the public sector.

Certainly in theory performance-related pay can play a helpful role in making individuals feel more accountable for what they do by virtue of being judged very personally and specifically for the contribution they make. However, the absence of many examples where it has worked in the public sector suggests that in practice this is not easy to achieve.

Creating accountability in a partnership

Working in partnership is a key element of delivery in many areas of the public sector. And if it is hard to achieve accountability within one organization, it can be exponentially harder to achieve it within a partnership. How can you ensure that different organizations over whom you have no direct control feel accountable for doing things well?

There is no shortage of quotes from the people I interviewed which are sceptical about the effectiveness of partnerships between public sector bodies. 'Tony [Blair] tried to get partnerships to work, for example in the area of crime', says Jonathan Powell. 'But there is no system for holding people to account because they just say it is not their responsibility.' Robin Butler echoes this: 'True accountability always comes in a silo – partnerships don't really work.'

And Charles Guthrie, the former Chief of Defence Staff, offers support for this point of view from a different part of the public sector altogether: 'Coalition forces always work badly', says Charles Guthrie. 'When you are in a place like Afghanistan, you have got 37 different nations with different agendas and levels of commitment. And all those nations first of all take orders from their national capitals, not from the commanding officer. So the Germans will only stay in the safest areas and won't really take any offensive action, they might just as well not be there actually except for political reasons.'

These quotes are striking because so much of the language and policy within the public sector is based around partnership working. But whether or not they are a good structure for delivering services, most public sector managers will find themselves working in partnerships in some form and most will find accountability hard to establish within them, even within the very strict command and control of a military operation.

So what can be done?

- **Learn how to disagree.** 'Too often people delude themselves into thinking "we have a system, we are chasing the same goal" when in fact they are not', says former Chief Constable Geoffrey Dear. 'You will almost certainly have very different objectives from your partners and it is sensible to bottom them out from the start and expect to disagree with each other on some of them.'

- **Spend more, not less, time on making them work.** It is much harder to get a partnership project to work than one within your own organization. It therefore follows that you should spend more time with your partnership than on similar projects, not less. Instead, it is easy for partnerships and the time you invest getting them to work to be marginalized. If it is important enough to do in partnership then it is worth doing properly.

- **Invest time in building up trust.** You are less likely to trust people you do not know well. When he was Mayor of London, Ken Livingstone would have one informal meeting a month – no notes, no staff – with the commissioner of the Metropolitan Police. This allowed them to build a relationship which made it easier for them to act quickly and get things done because they were not second guessing each other.

This investment of time is particularly important when the partnerships may not be instinctively compatible. 'Robin Cook, Clare Short, George Robertson and myself met frequently to discuss policy on Kosovo or Bosnia', says Charles Guthrie. 'We all came at it from different angles and with different personalities. It was particularly difficult because Robin and Clare disliked each other, but actually they were both nice people. It worked for me because I got on very well with them both and put a lot of effort into the relationships. Of course it helped that I was on the ground and probably knew more about it then they did but it also took time and chemistry. We were able to move forward together but it can be hard.'

Summary

There are some good reasons why managerial accountability is so elusive in the public sector:

- Political accountability softens the demand for managerial accountability.

- The quality of an individual's performance may not directly affect the quality of the results achieved.

- It is difficult either to observe directly what public servants are doing or to assess what they achieve – and sometimes both.

The best ways to overcome these challenges are:

- Embrace peer pressure and best practice. Relevant comparisons do improve accountability and performance. The availability of this data is a huge advantage for public sector managers.

- Get people as close as possible to the areas they are affecting. Make the accountability as personal as it can be.

- Establish a clear narrative. It will be particularly effective if it is also inspiring – and given the important work most areas of the public sector do, that should be easy to achieve.

Notes

1 Melanie Phillips, *Daily Mail*, 15 December 2008.

2 Calculations based on figures taken from the CIPD Resourcing and Talent Planning Surveys, 2009–2012.

3 Capability Review of the Home Office, July 2006, p 9.

4 Capability Review of the Department for International Development, March 2007, p 10.

5 They were right to be concerned; progress on Millennium Development Goals, particularly around infant mortality and maternal health, is not on track to meet the 2015 targets.

6 Of course, another interpretation is that DfID was setting itself deliberately ambitious targets so it was unsurprising that it failed to meet them.

7 James Q Wilson, *Bureaucracy: What government agencies do and why they do it* (Basic Books, New York, 1989), pp 158–71.

8 List taken from the Effective Services Delivery (ESD) Toolkit (http://esd4you.esd.org.uk/); the analysis (by me) is not a perfect science, particularly as increasingly outcomes in the public sector are based on measurable public opinion surveys. Nonetheless, even with the most generous interpretation most outcomes and most outputs remain immeasurable.

9 Rudolph Giuliani, *Leadership* (Miramax, New York, 2005), p 34.

Managing target setting

03

> "Targets are a waste of time and symptomatic of people who haven't run anything.
>
> **KEN LIVINGSTONE**

> Targets in one form or another are... both necessary and beneficial.
>
> **MICHAEL BARBER**

> Target use is a dangerous thing, but the truth is that if you don't have targets it's worse.
>
> **CHARLES CLARKE**

Targets are one way of making people feel accountable but they are such a large, complex, and – as the quotes above imply – controversial topic that they merit a chapter to themselves. This chapter sets out:

- the challenges of setting good targets in the public sector;
- why managers should avoid setting targets where possible, and how they can do so;
- tips for setting sensible targets when they need to be set.

Introduction – to target or not to target

Speak to any member of the last Labour Government about the NHS and before long you may find yourself talking about targets. Most likely you will hear about the success in meeting the demanding targets that were set around waiting times – for example that nobody should wait more than 12 weeks for treatment on the NHS or that nobody should wait more than 4 hours in A&E before they are seen. 'Targets work', says former Labour Cabinet Minister James Purnell. 'The targets we set in the English health service mean that it is now better than its Scottish and Welsh counterparts.'[1]

But speak to the doctors and nurses who were charged with meeting these targets and you will often get a different account. Here is one doctor's account:

> The four-hour wait has decimated A&E as a speciality. You have
> matrons jumping up and down worried that a patient will breach
> [miss the four-hour target]. The impact is that patients get passed
> from pillar to post and aren't dealt with in a sensible way. People
> can be so obsessed by measuring things that they lose sight of exactly
> why they are trying to measure them.

Or as a senior cardiologist put it to me: 'Targets have distorted a commonsense approach to the management of the health service.'

Without the simplicity of a bottom line, the public sector is under pressure to find other ways of demonstrating how it is performing. 'Sometimes we hide away and have this view that it's all too vague but you should always try your hardest to make it specific', says Gus O'Donnell, applying a little more of this pressure. Targets are an understandable response. They can also appear to be a useful way for managers to bring focus to particular areas and motivate employees. But they are often contentious – even in the case of an ostensibly successful target like the NHS waiting list – and can sometimes go badly wrong.

The consequences of bad targets

Consider the following conversation. On one side is a customer who needs his telephone line fixed. On the other is the customer service representative who is trying to help:

'Yes, we can arrange for an engineer to come to your house. He will be there within six days and he'll come on Friday morning at 10 o'clock.'

'That's pretty good – is that appointment going to be kept?'

'No, it's not.'

'Oh. Why not?'

'Well, you see, the engineers are currently so busy that they're working nine days ahead so what will happen is we'll have to phone the day before and rearrange the appointment.'

'Well, why don't you just give me a time that you think they can make?'

'Because we have a target that says people must be given an appointment within six days.'

It is easy to see how this target – used in the past by a telecoms company – may have come about. Why shouldn't customers be guaranteed service within a fixed time period? Six days sounds reasonable. Yet this innocent-sounding target leads to patently ludicrous behaviour which has a profound impact on the organization. Customers become angry and frustrated. Staff become embarrassed and weighed down with unnecessary work. Perhaps most significantly, managers fail to tackle the key issues because as far as they can see their targets are being met.

There are many such examples of poor targets leading to poor consequences. In the private sector these usually involve revenues and profits. The most high profile is the dance that takes place involving public companies and City analysts. City analysts start by predicting the range of profits they think a company will deliver – in effect a target for that company. In the run-up to the results, speculation will then revolve around the extent to which a company has met these expectations. As a chief executive you certainly would not want to underperform against them. In fact, if you had exceeded them by a large amount you might well want to hold something back in order to get next year's sales off to a good start. These targets can drive the presentation of results and can get in the way of a straightforward assessment of how the business has been performing and will perform.

Take the story of Rentokil and Sir Clive Thompson. During the time that Sir Clive was Chief Executive of Rentokil he became known as 'Mr Twenty Per Cent' because every year, with monotonous regularity, he set – and achieved – the target of increasing Rentokil's profits by at least 20 per cent. The City lauded him for this phenomenal achievement and during the first 10 years of his spell as chief executive Rentokil grew dramatically. Defenders of targets would say that Sir Clive's 20 per cent target galvanized his staff and imbued investors and analysts with the confidence to back the business. Opponents would say that Sir Clive could and should have achieved these objectives by different means and that the public commitment to this target put himself and the business under an unnecessary and unhelpful level of pressure.

What happened? After a downturn in trading, Sir Clive was forced out. The new chief executive and chairman said. 'Our review [of the business] has shown how the pressures – both internal and external – to meet [City] expectations led to management prioritization of very short-term goals. Prices were pushed to unsustainable levels. Costs were relentlessly taken out – often to the detriment of growing the business. Service quality was sacrificed. Sales efforts were impeded. As budgets became ever more unrealistic, so morale dropped and the focus became ever more short term.' No wonder Sir Clive ended up renouncing his 'Mr Twenty Per Cent' tag in favour of 'Mr Sustainably Outperform'.[2]

The public sector has no shortage of poor targets leading to poor outcomes. For example, in the RAF pilots are expected to fly a certain number of hours every year as training. It is important that you hit the target number of hours because this is tied to your progress and your budget. 'If you appear to achieve what you need to with only 95 per cent of the flying time then your budget will be cut', explains a recently retired fighter pilot. 'You can understand why they came up with this target. It is a simple way for us to explain to the Treasury what they are getting for their money. But it's too crude. What matters is not the number of hours you fly but the quality and variety. You could meet this target by flying at night back and forth in a straight line between Marham and Akrotiri but it wouldn't make you a better pilot.'

This is not a new problem. During his stewardship of the Federal Bureau of Investigation (FBI), J Edgar Hoover was determined to demonstrate the effectiveness of the agency to the public. He thought that making large numbers of arrests would be one way of doing so. To meet these targets his agents put their ingenuity and time into trying to deliver arrests rather than prevent crime. For example, they would boost the number of fugitives they arrested by targeting deserters from the armed forces – usually easy to track down and deal with – rather than dealing with the most dangerous and time-consuming fugitives. This pursuit of arrests culminated in the 1970s when 60 per cent of the cases the FBI presented to local US attorneys were being declined, often because the case was deemed too trivial to warrant prosecution.[3]

During my interview with David Normington, who at the time was Permanent Secretary at the Home Office, there was an echo of precisely this challenge. 'We moved from volume targets in 2004,' he recalled, 'to measuring serious and organized crime in 2008. We still measure volume crime, of course, but there were some very specific targets of volume crime which the police might have followed slavishly when you might want more resources to be focused on the serious end of crime.'

The consequences of bad targets would matter little if it were easily possible to set the right targets in the first place. But it is not.

The four pitfalls which make setting good targets virtually impossible

Here are the four most common pitfalls associated with setting targets:

1 **Picking the right indicator:** when the telecoms company chose to focus on the time taken to contact a customer, or when Hoover focused on volumes of crime, they were starting in the wrong place. The indicators they chose to focus on and set targets around were not the areas that would lead them to the outcomes that really mattered.

2 **Picking the right number:** how did Blair's government decide that the target for literacy among 11-year-olds – one of their most high-profile targets – should be 80 per cent? And not 79? Or 81? Did they make an assessment of what might realistically be achieved given the resources available and the current status of literacy in the UK? Not exactly. In the words of Michael Barber, 'We had little data to go on but plumped for an ambitious 80 per cent.' And what happened next? Did the politicians forensically challenge Barber about the basis for this ambitious target? Again, not exactly. When the policy was put before the prime minister, Barber reports: 'Blair asked whether we were sure the 80 per cent target would be met and everyone went silent and looked at me.'[4] Once Barber gave that assurance, the target became set in stone.

   How could something so important be done in such an arbitrary way? Perhaps because there is no good way to pick a number. Just think about the numerical targets you have been involved with. How much confidence have you had in their robustness? How much time have you spent revising them halfway through the year when things have not turned out as planned? I've certainly wasted time desperately trying to meet impossible numerical targets, putting together excuses as to why I've not met them or else re-forecasting the wildly inaccurate ones that I've set for others.

   These numbers matter. People will invest resources and take decisions in their quest to meet them. So it also matters that they are right – not too ambitious and not too easy. And yet there is no methodology which can pick the right number consistently.

3 **Understanding the impact of the target on the rest of the organization:** the focus on short-term profit in Rentokil had a knock-on impact on their service quality as they cut corners to

save money and meet short-term financial targets. Focusing on volumes of crime may have affected the Home Office's investment in more serious crime. By focusing on one target, you are effectively prioritizing one area over another. As a result there may be less attention paid to a particular business opportunity, to an area of the back office, or to a particular customer segment. It is important to have a clear view of the trade-offs involved – and very hard to do in large, complex organizations.

4 **Trusting the data:** can you really tell from the numbers whether the target has been hit? There are two issues here. First of all, how straightforward is the data to understand? The same data can be interpreted many different ways, whether it is financial analysts trying to make sense of a company's results, or policy analysts assessing the latest unemployment figures. If the data is ambiguous then it may be unwise to use it to set unambiguous targets. Secondly, is there enough genuinely independent auditing within the system? Chris Haskins vividly describes the impact that a lack of such independence can have, drawing from his experience on the board of the Yorkshire Regional Development Agency:[5] 'We hit our targets easily because it is in everybody's interest to do so. It is in the interests of the minister because he can get up and say I hit the targets. It is in the interest of the civil servants because they do not want to upset the ministers and it is in the interest of the people at the bottom because that is what they are asked to do. And within that complex environment you can play so many games to reach the target.' The value of a target decreases enormously when it is possible to manipulate the data and when people have an incentive to do so.

Why it is even harder to get targets right in the public sector

As if the list above wasn't depressing enough for public sector managers attempting to set a target, there are three further challenges which make it more challenging for them than for their private sector counterparts.

Public visibility and accountability

'Last year,' thundered *The Sun* in an article entitled **B**lowing **B**ritish **C**ash, 'the BBC spent a staggering £32,500 on reception area flowers.' The article went on to chronicle how much had been spent on biscuits, bank charges, taxi fares and, of course, expenses.[6] But what the article failed to disclose was how much organizations similar in size to the BBC spend on flowers or biscuits. How much does News Corporation, *The Sun*'s parent company, spend on reception area flowers? Is the BBC really spending outrageously given its size and function? Impossible to say without context.

As a public sector manager you live with the knowledge that every bit of information about what you are doing is liable to public scrutiny. In some cases – as in *The Sun*'s article – this information will be wilfully misinterpreted. In other cases there may be public misunderstanding because what you are doing is not easily distilled into a neat target that can be quickly and straightforwardly understood. 'Publishing death rates from heart disease in hospitals is a potential disaster', says Michael Heseltine. 'The most difficult cases go to the most sophisticated and risk-taking surgeons, so they have higher death rates. Therefore if you publish a hospital death rate the public will draw the conclusion that they shouldn't go near these hospitals, which is ridiculous, because they probably have the best treatment there.'

This also affects how ambitiously a target might be set. Miss it and there is every chance you will get lambasted by the media. Set it too low and you might not achieve much. 'I think it's daft to set targets where you have a 100 per cent probability of meeting them', says Gus O'Donnell. 'Give me a target where we have, say, a 70 per cent probability of meeting it. The key thing is knowing what that probability is.' Even more punchy is James Purnell: 'Risk definition, and risk getting it wrong.' Whatever approach you take, the point is that in the public sector you also need to think hard about how the public and the media will react to hitting – or not hitting – the target. It is just one more layer of complexity which makes the task of coming up with sensible targets that much harder.

Negotiating with frontline professionals

If the potential for unfair external scrutiny is one additional challenge for managers, then another is the internal involvement of frontline professionals.

There is a revealing scene in the 2007 BBC television series *Can Gerry Robinson Fix the NHS?* The premise of the programme is that Robinson, a successful, charismatic businessman, will be parachuted in to fix a hospital in Rotherham. In this particular scene he is running a workshop with the consultants at the hospital. He is using the workshop to pass on some suggestions, made by the hospital managers, which would improve the efficiency of the operating theatres. 'With respect, Gerry,' says one consultant, 'I've got five PhDs and most of these managers have barely got five GCSEs. What can they tell me?' Imagine the task of being the hospital manager trying to negotiate targets with that person.

Of course, many private sector businesses operate within such a structure of managers and professionals. Journalists will often complain about the commercial demands placed on them by their managers and proprietors. Many managers rely on the work of engineers and research scientists to create the value on which they build their businesses.

But it is arguably not as extreme as the public sector. First of all, there are many more professionals involved – police officers, doctors, nurses, soldiers, social workers, planners... the list goes on. Secondly, these professionals can go to the media for a sympathetic hearing when they disagree with what the managers are asking them to do. Soldiers complain about lack of equipment, nurses that they are overworked, police officers that they are being asked to do too much paperwork and so on. Thirdly, these professionals may feel a greater loyalty to, and respect for, their profession than to the organization (and the managers) for whom they work. Doctors will, quite reasonably, feel that they are there to serve patients no matter what structure fits around them or who is administering it.

In most cases managers and frontline professionals work very well together – and so they should. The manager brings an overview of budgets, demands and even the political context to the task of setting targets. The frontline professional brings the perspective of what is and is not deliverable on the ground. Both perspectives are required to reach the best targets. But the need to have these discussions and to reach sensible compromises without the straightforward hierarchy enjoyed by private sector managers can add complexity to the process of setting targets.

Defining and measuring outcomes

The final challenge once again stems from the lack of a single simple-to-measure success criterion. When Richard Wilson was Cabinet Secretary it was his happy duty to pass on to the prime minister a game which had been mischievously devised as a present for him, called Targetopoly. As the name suggests, the aim of this one-off game was to go round and round the board gradually knocking off all your targets. The not so hidden message of the gift was that it was quite possible to hit your targets and not achieve anything.

Certainly the task of setting targets in the public sector is not made any easier by the complexity of what it is trying to achieve. For some outcomes – like happiness – it is just very hard to find anything sensible to measure. In other areas, the relationship between what you can measure, the outputs, and what you want to achieve, the outcomes, is far from clear.

Earlier on, I mentioned how difficult it is to come up with a method of evaluating planning decisions. The main outcome we want from this service is, obviously, excellent planning decisions. But how do you judge those and how do you set targets for them? For a number of years, the key target for planning officers has been the speed at which they process planning applications. Although it is helpful to have an efficient process, this target does nothing to promote the quality of the planning decisions. Indeed, forcing planning officers to focus on the speed of the process risks taking their eye off the most important element of their job – getting the decision right.

There is an even more complex challenge in the area of child protection. Again it is easy to suggest an overall outcome – that all children live fulfilling childhoods and go on to lead fulfilling adult lives. The trouble is that from a management point of view this outcome does not help much. You cannot manage a department based on what might happen in 5 or 10 years' time. So instead targets are produced around more measurable outputs such as the number of children who appear on the child protection register. 'You could argue,' says Brian Dinsdale, 'that with a large child protection register the council is being very robust in seeking out problems and recording them. But you could also argue that fewer on the register might mean that their prevention services are being effective.' In a service where so much depends on the judgement of complex human situations by professional social workers, it is incredibly difficult to come up with sensible targets.

Crime presents a similarly complex challenge. Between 1988 and 2008, crime in all categories almost halved. And yet fear of crime has gone up or remained the same.[7] In one sense – and the most important sense – the police have performed terrifically well. But in another sense, if people still feel as nervous about crime as they ever did, then they have only partially achieved the desired outcome. After all, fear of crime does have a very real impact on the way people behave and the quality of life they lead. This is also a shame for the police as it means that they have not got the credit they deserve. By halving crime they have achieved that rarely sighted but often cited public sector phenomenon of transformation.

The point to draw from this example, as from the others in this section, is that the complexity of so much of the public sector makes all four of the pitfalls involved in setting targets – indicator, target, the impact, the data – exponentially harder.

So what should you do about targets?

Lord, make me chaste – but not yet. ST AUGUSTINE

The intellectual argument for not having targets is every bit as strong as St Augustine found the argument for chastity. It is almost impossible to set the right target and the consequences of setting the wrong one might be significant. For public sector managers the impossibility and consequences are even more significant than for their private sector counterparts.

The good news is that managers should be able to achieve the benefits that targets bring – focus and motivation – by using far less risky management tools. The less good news is that most managers will still feel the need to use targets and often for good reasons. So let's first look at the chaste alternative to setting targets before exploring the moments when it may be right to yield to temptation.

Aspiring to chastity – no targets, lots of data

"*You don't need targets, you just need to know how much you're spending and whether or not you're providing a good service.* NIGEL LAWSON

The ideal scenario for managers is to have timely, accurate data on all key aspects of your organization. Add in the public sector bonus of having access to the same data from your peer group and you really can luxuriate in management clover. Where you spot discrepancies either with your previous performance or with the current performance of a peer, you can dive in to find out what is going on. Good performance should be praised to the skies. Poor performance should be identified and managed. You avoid the inflexibility of setting targets, not to mention saving the enormous amount of time and energy spent setting them.

Ken Livingstone takes this approach. In his management of Transport for London he regularly reviewed reams of data about transport times, costs and customer satisfaction, but he never set targets. 'I never said by year X I want this many people using the route or this much money. Because over 10 years the number of people riding one route might go up by 70 per cent and another by 10 per cent for all sorts of reasons. If I set a target the people running the buses are going to focus on achieving that target instead of running a good service. You just can't say you'll have an arbitrary target.' Ian Blair, Commissioner of the Metropolitan Police during Livingstone's mayoralty, confirms this view of the data-driven Livingstone: 'Ken had an extraordinary grasp of detail. I hardly ever saw him speak from notes, though he would reel off lists of statistics.'[8] For Livingstone, when either his instincts or the data suggested that there might be an issue, he would wade in. He therefore lives up to his 'targets are a waste of time' mantra – with one notable exception which I will come on to later.

The best example of this approach I've come across is the Compstat system developed while Giuliani was Mayor of New York,[9] which is similar to the system now used by the London Metropolitan Police described by Helen Millichap in the last chapter. Crime statistics were collected every day and analysed centrally. Regular meetings would be held, with this data enabling them to ask questions like 'Why are car thefts down 20 per cent citywide but up 10 per cent in your area?' In Giuliani's words, 'we used that data to hold each borough command's feet to the fire'. He also required the entire central staff of the precinct to be present: 'It's much tougher to say, for example, that you don't have fresh numbers because the computer guy hasn't up-dated the software when the computer guy in question is standing right next to you.' In Giuliani's words, 'we used that data to hold each borough command's feet to the fire'. Obviously, such data need not be used in such a confrontational manner by all managers.

This example shows the key strength that public sector managers have in managing without targets – and also their key weakness. The strength is, of course, the access to comparative data. Because Giuliani could compare what was happening in different areas of the city, he was able to manage his priorities down to a very detailed level. The weakness is getting access to comparative data. Compstat works because it is able to produce almost real-time data on crimes through-out New York City. Although many parts of the public sector do have good comparative data, many do not. Either their data is not appro-priate for real-time capture or else the systems to record it accurately enough are not in place.

For those who do have good comparative data, one side effect of using it as a management tool is that you do indirectly create targets. Between 2008 and 2011, all English local authorities were measured against 198 indicators. This was a wide-ranging list and included indicators such as the number of people using libraries and the number of obese children in primary schools. The very act of measuring and then publishing these indicators created implicit targets for local authorities as they attempted to outperform each other. 'We always demand two things', said Paul Martin to me at the time. 'First of all that every indicator is higher than the previous year and secondly that we go on improving until we are in the top quartile among local authorities.'

When is it acceptable to yield to temptation

Sometimes it is hard to avoid the temptation of using targets. They can be comforting to customers and managers alike. They can be particularly comforting when you don't have reliable comparative data against which to benchmark your performance. And they can also be used when a particular service area is so straightforward that there is little danger of falling into any of the pitfalls outlined above. Setting a target for the percentage of invoices you pay within 30 days might be an example of one such straightforward area.

There are two further circumstances in which it may be entirely sensible to have targets. First of all, to achieve something radical, on 25th May 1961 President Kennedy made the following pledge: 'I believe that this nation should commit itself to achieving the goal, before this decade is out, of landing a man on the moon and returning him safely to the earth.' Putting a man on the moon (and returning him safely to earth) within a decade certainly counts as a radical, almost surreal, target. When he set this target Kennedy had no idea whether it would be possible to achieve. But by making this commitment publicly and tying his reputation to it, the president was making it sound real and achievable. On a practical level he was also giving NASA a very public mandate to demand the resources and the support they needed to make it happen. And of course it did happen.

Closer to home in all sorts of ways, Ken Livingstone did something similar with the London Congestion Charge. He set a clear goal – to deliver the congestion charge system – and a date by which it had to be delivered.

Would either of these things have happened without a time-bound target in place? Well, possibly. But the public commitment to such ambitious targets must have helped.

Radical targets can also have an impact at a more operational level. 'When I was a detective inspector a new target came in to ensure that 70–80 per cent of reported domestic violence incidents resulted in arrests', says Detective Superintendant Millichap. 'In my view, having that target was the single most important thing that changed the way this organization dealt with domestic violence. It forced people to change the way they did things so that it became routine for arrests to be made. It encourages an officer who is very busy to knock on an extra door five minutes away because a suspect might be there. Without a corporate target you would not have got that change in the mindset.'

Tony Blair also loved a radical target. Some he achieved, such as the 12-week waiting list and the increase in NHS spending to European levels. Others, such as his target to remove child poverty by 2020 or halve teenage pregnancy by 2012, have been less successful. Blair would no doubt argue that by setting these radical targets he achieved momentum in those areas more quickly than an incremental approach would have done and that they encouraged innovation.

A junior NHS manager recalled the impact of being on the receiving end of one of the demanding targets set by the Blair government:

> I was managing a urology department when the government brought in the target to bring waiting times for operations down to 12 months. The consultants hated this, partly because they didn't want to change and partly because there was funding set aside to operate on patients that breached the target which was used to pay the consultants to operate on these patients in the private sector, so they had a negative incentive to change. So I sat down and worked through the numbers using their data and presented them with some choices as to how we could meet this target. The result was that we restructured the rota and the way the urology department was organized.

The second circumstance in which setting a target may be justifiable is, if there is a need to reassure or impress the public in a specific area.

On 20 March 2002, Tony Blair chaired a meeting of COBRA – the Cabinet Office Emergency Committee. This meeting had not been prompted by a conventional crisis such as a foreign invasion or a health scare. It had been prompted by a sharp rise in street crime which was dominating the media and affecting public confidence. Treating it as an emergency was one way of reassuring the public that something was being done. The other was to set a target. In this case, Blair agreed with the police chiefs that by September of that year they would bring street crime back to the levels of the previous year.

Managerially, this was a classically terrible target. The level selected was arbitrary – simply a return to the previous levels. There was no evidence that any robust analysis was done to determine the resources required to deliver it or the knock-on impact it would have on the other responsibilities of the police. And the target did not deal with the underlying issues that were causing these crimes in the first place. But it did show the public that the government were taking this issue seriously and it did result in a sharp fall in knife crime. Politically, it was a huge success.

In a democratic environment there are many such targets, often in politically sensitive areas such as crime or health. We can see this, for example, in the efforts of the Coalition Government to devise targets for the number of immigrants that the UK will accept. 'One of the things you've got to do in the public sector is produce targets which have salience with the public', says Michael Barber. 'You're saying to people: yes, we took your taxes and we promised you that we were going to change the system, and look, we've changed it in ways that we know you care about. We got criticized quite a bit for health waiting times, but we knew that the public really cared about them. They hated waiting four hours in A&E, or a year for a hip replacement. We felt we had a mandate to change a national system so we needed to define a national vision of how it would be different.'

But even in these instances – the radical target or the publicly reassuring target – it can be worth challenging the need to set a specific number. 'You don't always need a target,' acknowledges Michael

Barber, 'but you do need to know what part of the world you are try-ing to change and how you want to change it.'

Further tips for setting targets and picking indicators

Although this chapter has encouraged you, I hope, to consider targets as guilty until proved innocent, here is some advice for the times when you do find yourself needing to set them. Much of this advice applies equally to the more sensible practice of identifying which indicators you want to monitor.

Devolve responsibility for setting targets as close to the frontline as possible

When Robert Naylor became Chief Executive of East Birmingham Hospital in 1985 he took over a demoralized and financially challenged organization. Indeed, there were even rumours that the hospital could be closed or at least downgraded. 'The most important thing I did to turn things round was to engage the clinicians in the management process and give them the responsibility for managing services. You have to be quite brave to devolve but if you want to change the culture you need to do it.'

Many follow this approach. 'I've come to the conclusion,' says Richard Wilson, 'that you have to go back to local communities and make them responsible for setting their own targets and allocating resources.'

'Things ought to be organized as close to the front as you can get them organized,' says Robin Butler, 'so that people really are in touch with the things in their regions and they are not doing it from a distance.' Charles Clarke agrees: 'The more you say that the schools and the police have a certain amount of resources and targets that are set locally, the better it is and the more accountability you'll get in the process.' And so does Chris Haskins: 'At the end of the day you must leave it that the people at the sharp end who are actually delivering have ownership of those targets – they are their targets, not my targets.'

In short, devolving target setting to people on the frontline can help ensure that the targets are set sensibly and that people are committed to delivering them.

Or use data to challenge frontline professionals

But there is another point of view. Michael Barber makes the case for driving targets from the centre: 'There are two challenges I found when negotiating targets from the centre. First of all, sometimes the experts in a field know so much about the difficulties of getting things done that they lack ambition. The accumulated knowledge you get from being a professional can make you think "Oh, this is going to be too difficult." Secondly, you're also the people who are going to have to do it. So we [The Prime Minister's Delivery Unit] often injected ambition that was otherwise missing.'

The way that Barber and his colleagues did this was with data:

> When you are negotiating targets you need your negotiators to be really well briefed. Because the people at the local level will know more about their area or services than you can ever know. So when we were negotiating with local authorities about literacy and numeracy rates, for example, I used to have a session 24 hours before briefing the 30 or so people who were doing the negotiations in the school districts and we would go through the data. The people doing the negotiation with Wigan would know which quintile Wigan was in and they would know the performance of the boroughs in the country who were similar to Wigan. This meant they could say to Wigan 'Hang on a minute. You're saying you can't achieve this but there are three other boroughs that are exactly like you and they are setting targets like this.'

Brian Dinsdale echoes this challenging approach: 'There is a view that the professional services should be the professional services and that's the end of it. And they decide when a road has been repaired properly and whether the road network is appropriate and whether the social care is being performed properly. I disagree. Our role is to challenge your performance against your peers, against whatever information is available, against what the organization and politicians think.' Andrew Turnbull has similar views. 'They [professional people] want to improve but they want to define what improvement means. It's up to the government and politicians to challenge whether these ideas fit with what the public wants and needs.'

Of course, these two approaches are not necessarily mutually exclusive. It can be possible to engage frontline professionals in the process of setting the target while providing robust challenge to them at the same time. But it may be useful to consider if your instincts lead you to emphasize one approach over the other and whether it could be useful to vary this.

Think about how you can develop counterfactuals

'We're trying to get ex-offenders into homes and jobs', says Gus O'Donnell. 'We can quantify where they are now and we can follow where they go. But actually in a downturn things are going to get worse no matter how brilliantly we do, so our success might simply be that it does not deteriorate as much as it would have done.'

O'Donnell is describing a challenge common to public sector managers when assessing the success or otherwise of their work. In a complex environment with multiple variables, how do you know whether you have made a difference? You might find yourself doing a fantastic job and yet, because of factors beyond your control (for example, the economic factors described above by O'Donnell), the performance indicators would suggest otherwise. And the reverse is true. You might find the dreadful work you are doing conveniently masked by some fortuitous circumstances. In either case, it is useful to have a way of assessing the counterfactual – what would have happened if you had not intervened.

This is much more easily said than done. It is very hard and potentially very expensive to develop counterfactuals. They might come in the form of a direct comparison with the performance of a peer organization. It might be that you can manage some form of controlled experiment,[10] provided it does not have a negative impact on those that are part of it. It may be that you can find some sort of historical comparison. It might simply be a case of evaluating it in this light, perhaps with the help of an external organization. But it is helpful to think about how you would go about developing counterfactuals as early as possible and to instil this thinking in your team and the people to whom you are accountable.

Think about what you need to measure, not what is easily available

You may hear managers say that the first thing they do is think about what can and what cannot be measured. This is sometimes not a sensible starting point. It leads to many of the unenviable targets and indicators already quoted in this chapter – planning application processing times, the time taken to respond to fix a telecom issue, even crime rates. Just because something is easy to measure does not mean it is necessarily useful. Far better to begin by thinking about what it is important to measure – the quality of a planning decision, or the satisfaction that a customer has with a service, or the fear of crime – and then work out how to measure it.

Summary

It is virtually impossible to set good targets, particularly in the public sector – and the consequences of getting them wrong can be damaging.

The best-case approach is to manage performance by monitoring data across a number of indicators, particularly if you can compare this with data from similar organizations. However, most managers will find some targets necessary in an imperfect world. In particular, it may be sensible to set targets when either you want to achieve something transformational or to increase public confidence in a particularly weak area.

> ## Checklist
>
> On your existing targets:
>
> - How clear are you about the knock-on impact they have on other parts of the service or organization?
>
> - Does it really need to be a target or could you achieve the same effect by monitoring the relevant performance data?
>
> - What is the risk that the data could be inaccurate, misinterpreted or manipulated?
>
> - Are you measuring what is easy to measure or what it would be most useful to measure?
>
> Generally:
>
> - Could you feasibly get better – more timely, more accurate, more easily comparable – data on the performance of your peers?
>
> - What are the really ambitious changes you want to achieve in your organization? Could setting a public target around that ambition be helpful?
>
> - Do your existing indicators and targets capture the important things or just the items that are easy to measure?
>
> - Can you demonstrate the impact you are having irrespective of external factors (ie what is the counterfactual)?

Notes

1 Support for this can be found in the Nuffield Trust Report: *Funding and Performance of Healthcare Systems in the Four Countries of the UK Before and After Devolution* (Nuffield Trust, London).

2 Dominic White, Rentokil Halfway Through Recovery (*Daily Telegraph*, 31 August 2001).

3 For more on this read James Q Wilson, *The Investigators: Managing FBI and narcotic agents* (Basic Books, New York, 1978), especially pp 128–32.

4 Michael Barber, *Instruction to Deliver: Fighting to transform Britain's public services* (Methuen, London, 2008), pp 28–32.

5 This was known as Yorkshire Forward.

6 *The Sun*, 16 March 2011.

7 *Crime in England and Wales 2008/09: Findings from the British Crime Survey and police recorded crime* (Home Office, London, July 2009); people usually recognize that crime has fallen in their neighbourhood – though not by as much as it has in reality – but think that it is just as bad as it ever was in the rest of the country.

8 Ian Blair, *Policing Controversy* (Profile Books, London, 2009), p 260.

9 For a full description of the system you could either read Giuliani's excellent book *Leadership* (Miramax, New York, 2005), paying particular attention to chapter four, or the account of his police chief, Bill Bratton, in his book *Turnaround: How America's top cop reversed the crime epidemic* (with Peter Knobler, Random House, New York, 1998); or you could watch series 3 of the HBO drama *The Wire* which compellingly brings to life the way that data can be used to drive changes in policing.

10 There is an excellent Cabinet Office report offering advice on how to run such experiments. Laura Haynes, Owain Service, Ben Goldacre and David Torgerson, *Test, Learn, Adapt: Developing public policy with randomised controlled trials* (Cabinet Office, London, June 2012).

Managing politicians

04

"It's like an arranged marriage – you need to work hard and not be too judgemental on either side. HAYDEN PHILLIPS

When you work with politicians the unwritten rules of the workplace are thrown away. GILL RIDER

This chapter explores how you can get the most out of your relationships with politicians. The questions it deals with are:

- How do you establish trust with politicians?
- How do you define your respective roles?
- How do you challenge politicians?
- How do you use politicians to help you do your job more effectively?

Introduction – the challenges of arranged marriages

Viewed from a management perspective, Cabinet reshuffles are extraordinary. Within a few hours, the leadership of some of the most important, complex organizations in Britain changes hands. It can be a chaotic process relying as much on chance and political calculation as on suitability for the posts available. Jonathan Powell vividly describes the twists and turns of a reshuffle in 2006: 'Tony saw Charles

[Clarke] and offered him Defence or DTI instead [of the Foreign Office], but he declined... Our hopes of him as a counterweight to Gordon Brown were finished. We looked desperately for a replacement... We nearly opted for David Milliband... Putting him in that position would have made him a target for the Gordon Brown death machine. So instead we chose Margaret Beckett.'[1]

Out of such chaos (and admittedly some appointments take place in a slightly more orderly fashion) begins the arranged marriage between politicians and their managers. This relationship represents perhaps the most tangible difference between the public and the private sector. No private sector manager has a democratically elected politician as their boss. This has some substantive consequences.

Politicians have different experiences and skills from public sector managers

In most professions the people who get to the top will have an understanding of how their organization works because they will have worked their way up through the organization or something like it. Not in the public sector.

'When New Labour came to power, the incoming ministers, with some honourable exceptions, had no idea what management was', says John Monks, the former General Secretary of the TUC. 'They expected to be able to say something and that it would happen.' Tony Blair vented his frustration with this situation when he complained about the scars on his back after spending the first two years of his premiership trying in vain to reform the civil service. As a barrister, Blair had little experience of management before he became Prime Minister. In this he is not alone.

'Politicians don't know much about management really', says former BP Chief Executive John Browne. 'At best they've either had experience as a non-executive director or they've built their own small business but this does not prepare them for running a government department.'

Instead of management experience the skills and experience of politicians will typically lie in policy making, communication and passing legislation. This can potentially create tensions right from the start of the relationship. 'It's the politicians who are accountable for managing change but the politicians can't themselves manage and generally speaking don't have any managerial skills', says Jonathan Powell. Politicians can be in the position of the homeowner who finds it hard to trust what a builder says about the costs and timings of putting up the new conservatory. If something goes wrong in the public sector, the accountable politician with little experience of delivery may struggle to tell whether public servants are doing their best, whether they are being incompetent or even whether they are being deliberately obstructive to protect their own interests.

Accountability is not aligned

In addition to having different skills, managers and their politicians can have different objectives. As a public servant the success of your career does not depend on the success of your political boss. Indeed, as a public servant your first duty is not to the politician but to the state. The neat theory is that politicians dictate the policy and the civil servants deliver it. Therefore, the politician is held accountable for the strategic success or failure, and the public servant is account-able for delivery. As discussed in Chapter 2 on accountability, in reality it is hard to draw such lines, with the result that responsibility even for operational matters may land at the feet of the politicians. Departments can fail spectacularly and publicly and the politician will resign whereas the civil servants will continue. Not only are public servants not therefore motivated exclusively by the success of their department, but in many ways this political system is designed to give public servants an incentive to keep a distance in case they get too closely identified with any particular politician or initiative. 'The same civil servant,' says Chris Haskins, 'who has been hugely loyal, supporting and implementing left-wing policies will the next day turn up, hugely loyal, supporting right-wing policies... it is designed so it is not accountable.'

This can lead to a delicate dynamic. 'Politicians have inbuilt para-noia', one middle manager said. 'They will quickly work out whether you are on their side or not because they come from a tribal mindset. Somebody told me that the ideal situation to be in is if a politician thinks that if you could speak your mind you would agree with them. You have to be careful when they test you out by provoking you into an argument or lead you to express opinions such as "this person/policy is useless, don't you think?"'

Politicians have little power to promote or fire

Typically the most powerful management tool is the ability to promote or sack individuals. Politicians do not usually have this power over their public servants. Of course, they can influence appointments and sometimes refuse candidates proposed to them, but their powers are limited, even if they are the Prime Minister. Jonathan Powell recalls an attempt to fire a permanent secretary who had been a disastrous failure. 'When we insisted that he should be sacked, it took the civil service two years and cost some millions of pounds.'[2]

On a practical level this means that the marriage is arranged on both sides; by and large the civil servants do not choose their minister, and the minister does not choose the civil servants. The same is true in local government.[3] At a more fundamental level, this affects the tone of the relationship. In a central government department the permanent secretary is the most important figure for the career of a civil servant. What he or she thinks – influenced, of course, by the minister at the time – will determine what happens in the careers of the civil servants within that department. For politicians this must feel frustrating.

The threat of publicity

In most jobs, if you disagree with, or perhaps even dislike, your boss then there is not much you can do about it. In the public sector, you can go to the media who will be delighted by the chance to write up what 'inside sources' have told them. Most often this will be in the form of anonymous leaks – sometimes via gossipy stories about how the politician throws things around the office, and sometimes via actual documents which highlight potentially embarrassing policies or processes. Occasionally this will take the form of a public stand. We often hear senior figures from the armed forces, or the police or the health sector, publicly questioning the decisions of their political masters. Of course, such leaks or public statements are rare but their potential adds some spice to the arranged marriage.

High and abrupt turnover

As well as all these challenges in the day-to-day relationship, there is the practical issue that the identity of your political partner may change rapidly and with very little notice. 'When I was in the Cabinet Office,' says Chris Haskins, 'I worked for five different ministers in five years. It is just a joke. So basically I cut through it all and said the only way I can make this work is to work for Blair.' Haskins' experience is not unusual. Naomi Eisenstadt, who ran the Sure Start Unit, provides a vivid account of the changes in the ministers she dealt with between 2003 and 2006: 'Charles Clarke... was replaced by Ruth Kelly. Baroness Ashton... [was] replaced by Lord Filkin. Margaret Hodge... was replaced by Beverley Hughes... David Blunkett replaced Andrew Smith... Ruth Kelly was replaced by Alan Johnson.' She further comments: 'Each one of these ministers was different not only in style but also very often in substance.'[4] Although bosses move around in the private sector, it does not happen as often or as suddenly as in the public sector. Also, politicians are usually – and understandably – keen to make a public impact in whatever role they take on, which can make life unpredictable for the people who work for them.

Of course, some of these differences may have positive effects too. There is less jostling between the politicians and their managers for positions. They are not competing for each other's roles and this removes a whole level of potential intrigue and tension present in some workplaces. In addition, and many would argue most importantly, public servants have the distance and objectivity necessary to 'speak truth unto power' and to protect the interests of the public at large. Since their careers are not directly dependent on politicians and their first loyalty is to the state, public servants should find it easier to give excellent, unbiased advice.

But in terms of the day-to-day relationship, these differences have the potential to make life more difficult. Certainly the cumulative impact of the different agendas, the different skills and the potential for leaks is that most politicians and public servants will enter into the arranged marriage with caution. Here is some advice on how to make the marriage work.

Some marriage guidance counselling

Try to understand their agenda both politically and personally

I think that being a minister in Britain is the most awful accountable job in the world. CHRIS HASKINS

I think a lot of politicians don't like officials because they don't really think the officials respect them. MICHAEL BICHARD

It is a tough life being a politician in power whether at a local or national level. You are on a short-term contract, you face daily public scrutiny and you are under pressure not just to deliver what you have promised but also to respond impressively to whatever may be thrown at you along the way.

Good public servants will understand all this and more. They need to understand their political priorities. There is, for example, no point spending time planning a round of nationalization for a politician who is hell-bent on privatization. They also need to understand them personally. 'Some civil servants are good at intellectually identifying the political dimension of a problem or an issue', says Michael Bichard. 'I think that isn't the same as really knowing what politicians want, fear, what their ambitions are, what keeps them awake at night, why they behave in a particular way, how important their constituency is.'

Paul Martin echoes this. 'Knowing members and where they're coming from and what they are interested in is really important. In some cases it is self-explanatory because of the role they have, but in other cases it isn't. Somebody's non-political experience may stimulate an interest that you didn't know about, an expertise that you weren't aware of or a different perspective that they bring to bear.' To this end Martin makes a point of getting to know all his 50 or so councillors personally. The relationship starts once they get elected and Martin ensures he has a one-to-one meeting with each new councillor.

This understanding should also extend to the way of working. A civil servant I spoke to recalled being impressed when Hazel Blears became Secretary of State at Communities and Local Government. She gave a speech in which she outlined not just what she wanted to achieve but also how her staff should communicate with her. She did not like policy documents, she told her staff. Anything that came across her desk needed to have real-life examples and evidence, otherwise she would not engage with it. For the civil servant this provided a useful instruction. Sometimes it is up to the public sector manager to work this out for themselves. When David Blunkett became his Secretary of State at the Education Department, Michael Bichard observed that every document sent up to his private office was immediately reduced to three or four sentences, presumably in part because the blind secretary of state did not want to have to absorb long documents. Bichard took the hint and soon this became the standard format for documents which went to the minister's private office.

As much as anything else these actions are about demonstrating that you respect the politician and the political process. 'If you despise politics then you are fated to be a bad public sector manager', says one manager. 'This is not because you need to have a sentimental respect for democratic processes but because ultimately you have to do what the politicians say, and if you do it half-heartedly you will not do it well.'

Most of my contact with politicians has been in local government where the calibre can vary enormously. While there are many excellent politicians, some are ill-equipped for the task because they lack the right skills, the commitment or in some cases simply the time. Yet rarely have I encountered a manager who is either implicitly or explicitly disrespectful whether in public or more informal meetings. 'I have always had huge respect for the politicians I've worked with', says Heather Rabbatts. 'They're doing something enormously difficult, don't get any real money for it and spend every hour of their free time trying to make a difference.'

The public servant who can demonstrate this sort of respect will find the relationship much easier to navigate.

Use politicians to do the things that you cannot

But politicians can also help you do your job better. 'The mindset I've had about politicians is that they are a fantastic resource', says Paul Martin. 'They can be utilized and marshalled for the benefit of the community. And I think politicians want to be seen in that way. They're not obstacles to be overcome or simply decision makers to be guided.' Martin often asks his politicians to test out ideas on their constituents or find out how they are feeling about different aspects of the council's service. This gives him invaluable immediate feedback. And he also uses them to help with the operational planning. Just as a business chief executive will ask plugged-in bankers how the City might react to a particular acquisition or round of fundraising, Martin also uses the councillors' expertise when he is thinking of new initiatives. The councillors will be much better placed to assess what people might think and also to help Martin work out how to present council plans to them in the most effective way.

Peter Rogers also takes advantage of the link that councillors have with the community. At Westminster City Council he made sure that once a year he would visit every ward with every local councillor. 'This meant that I was aware of what they felt as politicians about how the officers were dealing with them, but more than that it gave me a view of the quality of the services for real. The thing you learnt very quickly was that the power of the ward member to engage locally is as important as the leader's view at the top of the organization. And I think that is something that is missed with politics.'

From the political side of the fence Ken Livingstone certainly feels that he can bring inputs to decisions that his officials cannot. When he decided to go ahead with the congestion charge against the advice of everyone around him, one of the determining factors was his confidence that the public would support it. 'I've got what they don't have which is that I walk down the street and everyone tells me what they think.'

Paul Roberts learnt the hard way about the value of taking advantage of the access politicians have to their communities when he was Director of Education at Nottingham City Council. He faced one of the trickier challenges that education directors face – closing down a local school. 'Although the case I was putting was absolutely watertight in terms of facts, figures and the logical analysis, I didn't build adequate support for it internally with the politicians. There was a very public throwing out of my proposal with an overflowing public gallery baying for me.'

The next time he proposed that a school should be closed he made certain that the politicians were on side:

I laid out the facts and analysis [to the politicians] very early on and they were convinced. My relationship with them was strong and I pay complete tribute to the fact that my Chair of Education at the time insisted on doing the community meetings with me. He took political flak and we were seen shoulder to shoulder very visibly and he stuck with the decision. We would meet with those parents, initially very angry parents, on a very regular basis and hear their concerns about the closure and we would try and deal with them. It was a very properly politically led activity and worked brilliantly and I felt quite proud of that.

The politicians in this instance were better placed to make the case both because they had the links into the community and also because they were more used to engaging with their community.

How to challenge a politician

At the Department for Education Michael Bichard had an excellent relationship with his Secretary of State David Blunkett. But it was tested when the department lost a high-profile court case which many thought it should never have pursued in the first place. Bichard takes up the story:

David was door stepped by a journalist immediately after the case had finished and said that he had clearly received bad advice from his department and that he would have to look into it. People in the department were incensed and so I said to David, 'I'm sorry, I can't support you on this one. I'm going to have to write to you saying I've actually looked at the advice again and if I were giving you the advice I would have given you exactly the same advice. And I'm going to have to circulate that to the department.' Because we had the relationship we did, he said that he understood and probably shouldn't have said what he did.

Bichard felt it was crucial to do this for the message it sent to the department – namely that he would stand up to the minister if he thought the minister had got it wrong. 'And it did have a galvanizing effect in the department. People were watching this, one of those moments where people just watch and wait and see. Now let's see what the bastard does.'

Three things stand out from this episode. First of all, the importance of straightforward communications, between Bichard and Blunkett initially and then between Bichard and his department. The second is that Bichard's main motive in acting was to show his staff that there were circumstances in which it was right to stand up for them to the politicians. The third element is that he was able to handle the situation in this way at least partly because he already had a strong and trusting relationship with Blunkett.

Achieve clarity on choices and process, go for flexibility on roles

'The key role of officers,' says Merrick Cockell, the chair of the Local Government Association and a council leader for more than 10 years, 'is to push members to be clear about what they want, and in my experience most officers like this clarity.'

For Peter Rogers the budgeting process was the key moment to push for this clarity and get members to commit to what they wanted to achieve. 'You need to establish the principle that once the budget is agreed, you and the politicians are accountable for delivering it. If they come to you with things they wish they had put in there but aren't, you have to have a fairly robust conversation and say no unless they have worked out what will drop out and who is accountable for it.'

'What you have to make clear,' says Heather Rabbatts, 'is the process by which you made this allocation of resources because politicians have people coming through their door complaining about things. You need to make sure the conversations are about prioritization, not rationing. Sometimes it's about how you say no. The trick is to be a bit lateral and think of a way in which you can deliver what they want in some form.'

But while it is important to be clear about the choices made by politicians to ensure that things get delivered, it is much harder to be clear about roles. Let's go back to the theory that the politician sets the strategy and the public official delivers it. Many use a private sector analogy to describe this relationship: in this analogy the politician is the chair of the board responsible for the overall direction and the most senior official (eg the permanent secretary) is the chief executive who delivers it. But this doesn't work and Jonathan Powell explains why:

> In the private sector the CEO is going to be the one that has to go to the public meeting to justify to the shareholders whereas, in the case of politics, a politician has to do that... and that's what leads to a lot of trouble in government. You have to be careful because you don't want to draw lines too firmly around it because if you say we're just implementers, you tell us what you want to do, you can actually alienate the politicians and create the tensions you don't want to have. Equally, if you try and do everything you'll alienate them in another way.

Andrew Turnbull observed a curious but not uncommon subversion of this role on a visit to Barnsley Council. Because the politicians were closer to the day-to-day concerns of their constituents, they became involved in day-to-day issues of delivery. The officials, on the other hand, were at one remove and able to take a step back. Turnbull concluded that 'the chief executive had been setting the strategy and the members have been deciding whether Mrs Willis got Flat seven'. The mechanics of democracy had almost precisely reversed the conventional roles and responsibilities.

As a politician, Merrick Cockell recognizes that it can be hard to draw lines. 'Sometimes members think they can write a contract better than the officers because they've looked up the price of a whiteboard on the internet and seen that it's cheaper.' This, as Cockell implies, can be infuriating for public sector managers. But the advice for them is to be flexible when politicians delve into the operational side of things, though not about the choices that have been made. Politicians have different skills and experiences and so their input may be helpful. And in most instances their desire to get involved will be driven by what they perceive their constituents need. Indeed, Nick Walkley has found it helpful to be proactive in involving politicians. 'Every politician needs some delivery because actually you don't get into politics, particularly as a local politician, simply to think strategic thoughts. It's not a particularly fun way to spend your time. So the critical issue is to identify where their operational issues are and how to securely allow them some line of sight to them.'

For Robin Butler the flexibility emerges from a very human relationship. He recounted an occasion when Margaret Thatcher had stood by a civil servant who had made a mistake which embarrassed her publicly. 'It's not words, it's not even process. It is what happens at the moment when you are under fire and the person is there beside you.'

Summary

Politicians and their public servants have an unusual relationship because they typically have different backgrounds and their personal interests are not aligned. The relationship works best if public servants genuinely respect politicians (and show it) and if they can understand the personal and political agenda of their political bosses (and show it). It also helps to force the politicians to be clear about the choices they are making and clear about the implications of those choices. But it may not always be possible or desirable to be clear about the roles that politicians play.

Public servants should also use politicians and the access they have to citizens to get feedback on services and to test and 'sell' new ideas.

- Do you respect your politicians? Do your politicians think you respect them?

- Could you summarize their political agenda?

- Could you at any one moment articulate what their top three concerns are?

- How comfortable to you feel saying 'no' to your politicians?

- When did you last make use of your politicians? Are there any areas where their feedback would be useful or where you would like them to test new ideas?

Notes

1 Jonathan Powell, *The New Machiavelli: How to wield power in the modern world* (Vintage, London, 2011), p 146.

2 *The New Machiavelli*, p 76.

3 The exception in both central and local government is that the political leaders do appoint the top executive.

4 Naomi Eisenstadt, *Providing a Sure Start: How government discovered early childhood* (Policy Press, Bristol, 2011), p 88.

Managing people

05

"The public sector is largely about people. It is not about processes, it is not about factory machinery, it is not about the manufacturing of goods and sales invoices and all those things that come into so many other walks of life. If the people are right, then the service is right.
GEOFFREY DEAR

If Geoffrey Dear is correct, this may be the most important chapter in the book. Of course, many other parts of this book, particularly the chapter on accountability, touch on themes which affect the way you manage people. This chapter therefore focuses on three very practical aspects of management:

- **Assessment and development:** How do you know how well someone is performing? How do you translate this knowledge into meaningful and useful support? How do you have difficult conversations? How do you ensure not just that you give good appraisals, but that the people below you are giving good appraisals to their staff?

- **Underperformance:** How do you deal with extreme underperformance? How do you know the difference between someone who needs development and someone who will never be good enough?

- **Recruitment:** What qualities do you look for? What process do you go through? What questions do you ask?

Assessment and development – appraising the appraisal

Sitting in judgement on the performance of another human being is not the most comfortable thing in the world to do. This probably explains why we are often so bad at doing it. Many organizations will say that people are their number one priority and yet fail to assess and develop them effectively. Here is a test. Pick somebody at random and ask them to tell you their strengths, their weaknesses and what they are doing to improve their performance. In fact, better still, ask yourself these questions too.

The standard solution for assessment and development is, of course, the appraisal. This comes in a variety of forms and so for the purposes of this chapter my loose definition of an appraisal is a formal, regular process for giving people feedback. Everyone I spoke to used appraisals in some form. In my view they are a critical management tool – perhaps the most critical. If done well, they should support and improve the performance of individuals but they can also be a lever to drive the performance of an entire team or organization.

However, despite their ubiquity, there is some scepticism about their effectiveness. Some managers instinctively distrust a mechanized process for assessing people. 'It [assessing people] is what we all do every single day of our lives with everybody we meet', says one manager. 'So why do we pretend we don't have those skills as people and why do we set down a whole load of tick boxes and pretend that is a platform for our judgement?' Certainly appraisals have not always been done well. 'The problem used to be that appraisals were secret', says former Cabinet Secretary Richard Wilson. 'People weren't allowed to know what was said about them, and no one ever did an appraisal interview.' When another Cabinet Secretary, Gus O'Donnell, started in the civil service the appraisal was viewed almost as a publicly available reference document: 'People used to negotiate the words on their appraisal forms... they became pretty meaningless as a result... we didn't want to tell people to their face that they were underperforming.'

Things have probably got better but often the appraisal is still viewed with suspicion. Boxes are ticked, scores are given, project goals are muddled with personal development goals and a meeting is held in which meaningful and potentially awkward messages are avoided. 'Appraisals can hit the target and miss the point', says Ian Watmore.

There are some poor examples. 'People will treat appraisals as a process', a middle manager told me. 'They will say "This is as painful and boring for me as it is for you but we just have to do it."' I came across one department whose standard practice for meeting their corporate requirement for appraisals was to change the date on the previous year's appraisal and refile it as the new one. Sometimes they do not happen at all. University College London Hospitals (UCLH) employs more than 10,000 staff. Sixty-three per cent did not have an appraisal in 2009 and of those that did, only 25 per cent found them useful. In other words, fewer than 1 in 10 employees had useful appraisals. I suspect UCLH is unusual more because it has bothered to measure what happens on appraisals rather than for the results their survey shows.[1]

Bad practice around appraisals is not, of course, exclusive to the public sector. But the constraints under which the public sector operates can make it harder. Without easily measureable success criteria and without clear goals it can be difficult to tell how well an individual is performing. And in complex areas which require cooperation between different departments and organizations it can be even more difficult to work out the impact that individuals have had.

Assessment and development – how to deliver good appraisals

There is no excuse for not doing appraisals properly – people will leave organizations if they don't know how well or badly they are doing and you need proper appraisals to achieve this. JAN PARKINSON

Parkinson is right. Despite the challenges of giving appraisals in the public sector, there is no excuse for not doing them properly. Here are some tips for ensuring that you can do them properly.

Get evidence

It is impossible to give useful appraisals without good evidence. For a start, any feedback you do give will be harder for the appraisee to understand and act upon. Secondly, without evidence the quality of the feedback will almost inevitably be less good because it will be less well informed. Thirdly (and in my view most significantly), without strong evidence the appraiser may shy away from delivering the difficult but potentially most useful feedback; it can feel cavalier to criticize people unless you are sure of your ground and inhibiting to feel that you may have no credible response if you are asked to justify your criticism. But it is not just constructive negative feedback that suffers without evidence. Praise can sound hollow and fail to deliver the desired fillip unless backed up with relevant examples to show that the appraiser means it.

Good evidence is important for appraising people at every level. The Cabinet Secretary faces one of the toughest management challenges around. It is his task to assess the performance and help the development of 20 or so permanent secretaries. All of them (one would hope) are likely to be bright, sophisticated and ambitious – the sort of people who will require any criticism levelled at them to be well justified. Moreover, these are people with whom the Cabinet Secretary will not get the chance to spend enormous amounts of time. So how does he deal with this? Part of the answer is that he has independent evidence in the form of the capability reviews discussed earlier. These give him a basis for discussing with each of the permanent secretaries how well their individual departments are doing and what areas they could improve in. 'Before the capability reviews came in, I found it hard to give tough messages,' said Gus O'Donnell while he was Cabinet Secretary, 'but now I feel more confident about what I'm saying.'

Fortunately you do not need to be a cabinet secretary to get good evidence. There are a number of potential sources available for all managers.

Get hard data about the hard stuff

The public sector has a potentially vast resource of data available. This will cover performance not just in the appraisee's organization, but almost as significantly it will cover the performance of similar service areas in comparable organizations. Thus you can compare how much your neighbouring local authority has spent on care-home provision, or what has happened to rates of arrest for particular crimes or how quickly different transactions are processed. Such data provides a non-emotional evidence-driven basis for starting a meaningful discussion about performance.

Rigorously ask other people about the soft stuff

But performance data on its own does not provide a full picture of how well an individual is performing. In every type of organization, public and private, there are examples of poor employees and managers being flattered by good numbers and staff doing excellent work which is not reflected in results. There are so many variables, particularly in the public sector, which might affect what the performance numbers look like that to get a rounded sense of an individual, managers need to look elsewhere.

And obviously performance data does not capture the softer areas of a person's performance, for example the qualities of their communication, their analysis, their leadership or teamwork. The response to this is straightforward in theory and is well expressed by Richard Wilson: 'The only way to know whether or not you are doing a good job is to ask people systematically over a period of time.'

Of course, many organizations do this already through 360-degree feedback. In this process, the subject of the appraisal gets feedback on his or her performance from colleagues around, above and below them in the organization. But there is often scope to do it more thoroughly. One manager describes the 360-degree process in his organization: 'There is not a lot of time spent doing it. It is done by computer, and you're allowed to use 20 words under three or so different headings. It just isn't taken that seriously.' Based on the organizations I have seen, he is far from alone in having this experience. It is common for feedback obtained by the 360 to be patchy or superficial and very difficult to use meaningfully. Another common challenge is that people may not feel comfortable giving direct and blunt feedback, even anonymously, on their managers.

And there is one further challenge. Typically the input for 360-degree processes will come from colleagues within the organization. Yet for most public sector managers there will be many external people who are well placed to judge the quality of their work, particularly the external-facing areas which may not be visible to their colleagues. These will include suppliers, customers, citizens, partners, their counterparts in other public sector organizations and perhaps even parts of the media. These stakeholders may all have valid perspectives to offer about the performance of an individual and should be engaged in the process.

Above all, the key message is that managers should invest considerable time and energy in getting feedback from a variety of people about the performance of their staff to inform the appraisal. It should not be a half-hearted added extra but a full-blooded exercise which should drive the appraisal. It is worth the effort for public sector managers because in a working environment which lacks clear targets and goals, aggregating opinions systematically and consistently will be the best way to assess performance and provide meaningful feedback.

Make the most of your personal experience

Managers will also base their assessment of staff on the experiences they have had of working with them. This will happen instinctively for most, but it can be helpful to think more proactively. Specifically, it may be helpful to ask yourself two questions. First of all, are you using your everyday contact to full effect by capturing and in some instances immediately sharing feedback on performance with your staff? Secondly, are there opportunities you could create to observe your staff performing in situations in which you would not normally come across them?

Reviewing outputs is an obvious opportunity to gauge performance and offer feedback. Are forms accurately filled in? Are reports clearly written? Is the analysis sensible? Are presentations well set out? And can you see any trends in performance, either good or bad, which it might be helpful to feed back to the individual?

Observing people in action is also a rich source. No doubt there are a number of activities that you will automatically see your staff doing – attending meetings and perhaps giving presentations, depending on the role. But there may be others that you have not. Have you seen the way your staff interact with their customers? Or with their organizations? Or with their own direct reports? Have you seen them lead meetings?

Peter Rogers provides a good example of a proactive way of assessing performance. He says that at any time he likes to have a good view in his head of the abilities of the top 50 or 60 people in his organization. One of the ways he ensures this happens is by giving people a task – usually written – to do directly for him as soon as they join. 'If the person comes back and the quality of the work is good, the thought processes are good, the conclusions are good and it came in on time, then you know that you can trust that person for a series of jobs. If it is missing on one of those then you know that they have got a problem. And if it is missing on a number of them then you know that you have a real problem.'

So there are plenty of opportunities to get evidence on how people are performing in the workplace through your daily contact with them. The challenge is twofold: first of all, to make sure that these opportunities do materialize, and secondly, to use these moments to gather information about how people are performing in a way that can be fed back to them either immediately or in formal appraisals.

How do you appraise a Cabinet Secretary?

Gill Rider had the task of putting together appraisals for her boss Gus O'Donnell, the Cabinet Secretary. Her approach was to ask the Permanent Secretaries who all reported to O'Donnell two simple questions: What are the three things that he does well which you would like him to continue doing or do more? What are the three things that he does badly which you would like him to stop doing or do less of? This worked well. It is a relatively simple and unthreatening way for Permanent Secretaries to give feedback which produced useful and focused points for O'Donnell. 'It was particularly useful,' says Rider, 'for highlighting the things that Gus thought his colleagues valued but which weren't mentioned in their top three.'

If you don't have evidence, make the most of your hunches

In a perfect world all the activities described above will lead to insightful and helpful steers for the people you are managing. Every comment will be perfectly supported by spot-on examples demonstrating precisely the point you are trying to make. But more often than not – and no matter how much time you invest in gathering evidence – it can be tricky to support some of the subtler and more sensitive observations you might want to make.

One of the most valuable bits of advice that I have come across in the course of these interviews relates to this challenge. Paul Roberts takes appraisals very seriously. One of the rules he sets himself is that every appraisal should be challenging in some way for the appraisee. When he doesn't have evidence, this creates a problem.

He deals with this problem through informed speculation. Specifically he frames much of his informed speculation through saying: 'I don't have the evidence to back this up but my impression is that you are...' This, he says, serves as an unthreatening basis for having really good and useful discussions – and discussions that do not have to be recorded formally. 'If I relied totally on evidence for giving appraisals,' says Roberts, 'the feedback I give would be very limited. I find that the only way you can move people on is by getting past what you've got evidence for into some of the developmental issues.'

Tie appraisal objectives to the organization's objectives

Behind the evidence gathering lies the structure of the appraisal itself. What objectives are you assessing people against? Clearly it is important that these objectives are linked in some way to the objectives of the organization as a whole. But this can be hard to achieve in practice. Appraisal objectives can often be very general and test abstract qualities which have little to do with the desired outcome or customer experience. In larger organizations, there is also a danger that the understandable desire for consistency can lead to a standard template being applied broadly without enough thought about the different requirements for each area.

When Michael Bichard took over at the Benefits Agency he discovered that the Agency had the same appraisal system as the Department for Work and Pensions (DWP). This made no sense. Although the Agency was part of the DWP, the activities that the staff in benefits offices undertook were very different from those undertaken by civil servants sitting in Whitehall. And yet people delivering the services in the benefits office were being appraised on their performance in nebulous areas like flexibility and analysis. 'Well, your average punter at the Toxteth benefit office wasn't too interested in any of that', says Bichard. 'What they wanted was someone who was genuinely dedicated to improving the quality of the service that individual got, who treated them with respect and who was focused on the targets that those people care about, which were accuracy and speed.' Bichard spent six months working out what they wanted to achieve as an organization and then made sure that these goals, largely around better customer service, were reflected throughout the appraisal system.

Crucially, he also linked these objectives to promotions:

> There's no stronger message sent through any organization than promotion; the people who get promoted are noticed, the people who don't get promoted are noticed and people work out why. And if you've got someone who has a track record as an innovator, who's taken reasonable risks and maybe has had some failure, but has managed that to the best of their ability, who really is passionate about customers and clients, and this person doesn't get promoted, the rest of the organization spots it. So you've got to reward the things you say are important to you and do that through the appraisal.

Use your behaviour to support appraisals

As a manager there are many ways in which you can indirectly encourage a positive approach to appraisals above and beyond any formal processes you may have in place. This is particularly important if you manage large numbers of people. You may be able to manage the quality of the appraisals for your direct reports. But what about their direct reports and the ones below them? Using your behaviour to influence the culture around appraisals can be vital.

Earlier in this chapter I mentioned the surveys they use at UCLH to assess how often appraisals are conducted and how satisfied people are with them. Collecting and publishing this data is one way of setting expectations throughout the organization about the import-ance of appraisal. But Robert Naylor uses his own contact with staff to push the message home. 'When I speak to a ward sister I will take the opportunity to ask her how she is doing on her objectives this year. If she quotes me back different objectives to the ones set in the strategy then I know the team appraisals are not being done right.'

I interviewed Nick Walkley when he was Chief Executive at Barnet and he described how every week he would visit a different area of the organization for a session called 'Meet the Chief'. This was a chance for him to find out how that particular area was doing and to answer questions from the staff. But he also used the time to find out about appraisals. 'I ask the staff very direct questions about their experience of appraisals, questions about what issues have been iden-tified, how they are being picked up and fed upwards. It's never very scientific but it gives me a flavour of what they're experiencing of the management culture. And as you can imagine, everybody else in the organization hates it.'

He reinforced the importance of appraisals in other ways, too. 'If you walk around the organization the place is blitzed with posters and screensavers and not just the "you must do the appraisal" but also stories about what people have done as a result of having an appraisal, where people have moved and where they have been promoted.'

More formally, Geoffrey Dear would routinely challenge the ap-praisals given by members of his team when he felt that they were bland and unhelpful. 'I would call in supervisors and say: "Why is it that all your team are sheep and not a mixture of sheep and goats?" You actually have to confront them with the evidence that they arith-metically cannot have a team which is all of one type and has no distribution of talent.'

These conversations serve a number of purposes. They demon-strate that you as a manager value appraisals. This means that others will value them too. But they also provide a shorthand way of taking the temperature of what is happening in different parts of the organization. When Robert Naylor is asking the ward sister about her appraisal he is finding out not just how she is performing and how well the appraisal system is working, but also how well his strategy is being delivered on the ground.

It also demonstrates another advantage of the appraisal process, namely that it provides a common framework for starting conversations about performance with anyone in the organization. Rather than asking questions which are bland and unlikely to yield anything particularly insightful, managers can get into meaty issues almost immediately simply by asking 'how was your last appraisal?' and 'what are your key development points?'.

Train people to deliver effective appraisals

'Every Friday night my chief executive would pour his heart out to me for an hour and a half about how bloody useless his senior team was. And yet when it came to the performance reviews they all scored fours and fives because he would just back off.' Even at the highest levels – this quote is from the former chair of a large public sector body – people have difficulty giving effective appraisals. 'Some people are just uncomfortable with being leaders', one manager told me. 'They find praise patronizing and criticism too school-marmy. They need to change this.'

One solution is to buy in trainers to help managers give appraisals. 'We've done quite a bit of training about how to have those difficult conversations', says Nick Walkley. 'It has been well received and it helps. We're going to continue with it.' From the other side, one middle manager told me that she had invested in training her staff who were on the receiving end of appraisals. 'The coach encouraged my team to think hard about their development points before their appraisals so that they drive the process from the bottom up.'

This training does not necessarily have to be external. 'There is a very strong feedback culture in the RAF', a former squadron leader told me. 'I never had a problem delivering difficult messages in appraisals or being on the receiving end. Part of this is because we are used to doing it. After every training flight there is 360-degree feedback which is often robust. And my squadron are judged on the quality of the feedback they give me as the leader. If they don't pick up on something I've done badly, I'm unhappy with them.'

Helen Carter will occasionally coach her staff by using role-play to prepare for particularly difficult appraisals or performance issues. 'It can be strange at first and some people are uncomfortable with it but I always tell them that the real one can only be easier than the role-play. And it usually gives them confidence and ideas about how they might manage the discussion.'

Investing time or money in training people to give effective appraisals not only builds real skills, but it also sets expectations about the professionalism of the appraisal process throughout the organization. And, importantly, it is another way of helping people feel comfortable having honest conversations about performance.

Managing poor performance

Managing poor performance is the hardest part of the job.
HAYDEN PHILLIPS

Not many people relish dealing with poor performance. 'It is always a joy to do appraisals when people are doing well', says Heather Rabbatts. 'But with the ones who are not, you think "can I delay it?".' Charles Farr gives a vivid description of what giving difficult messages can be like. 'If you give people bad news [about their performance] the lights immediately start flashing and the emergency services arrive and you have to provide the medicine and the treatment.' So why and how do these and other successful managers do it?

Confront it

Managing people is all about having the difficult conversations. **GILL RIDER**

The overwhelming advice from the people I interviewed was that poor performance needs to be confronted no matter how unpleasant or time consuming it might be to do so. There are four key factors which can help push you to make the effort to have these difficult conversations:

1 **Remember that the other staff will probably welcome it.** 'In every single staff survey we have done,' says Charles Farr, 'more people complain about the way that underperformance is handled than almost anything else. And what they are complaining about is underperformance by others.' It can be frustrating to feel as if a colleague is getting away with doing a bad job: it affects the reputation of the team and can make the good performers feel underappreciated and sometimes overworked as they compensate for their colleague. 'People know who the weak links are within a team,' says Richard Wilson, 'and are usually grateful if they are dealt with by the management.'

2 **It will improve everyone's performance.** 'The culture is affected if you're sitting next to people who are underachievers and they are being allowed to get away with it', says one manager. Poor performance by an individual can affect not just the quality of what he or she does, but also the quality of the team's performance. Similarly, when poor performance is confronted it sends an indirect but powerful message about standards and expectations in the workplace.

3 **It will probably save you time and energy in the long run.** Poor performers can eat up management time and energy. Managers will find themselves correcting mistakes, investing time in development and simply worrying about how to handle the individual. And by not confronting poor performance, managers can be storing up longer-term issues. 'If you don't deal with it [poor performance],' says Nick Walkley, 'you will end up needing a much wider cultural change than just getting rid of a couple of poor performers because it will have embedded a whole series of other cultural and performance attitudes which will need to be rooted out as well.'

4 **It may not be as painful as you fear.** 'Poor feedback is rarely a surprise', says Helen Carter. 'And as long as it is constructive, most people recognize and are grateful for such honesty and the effort that you have put into giving it to them.' Richard Wilson echoes this: 'People usually know when they are underperforming and it is helpful to get it out in the open.'

An NHS manager recalls taking on the challenge of giving negative feedback to a much older and slightly prickly member of her team. 'The first time she screamed at me in the middle of the office but in the end she appreciated it because nobody had taken an interest in her before. I won her loyalty and respect for taking the trouble.' And, of course, confronting it may well be in the interests of the individual. 'We need to get better at managing performance and to my mind this is all about honesty', says Gus O'Donnell. 'The point we need to get across is that the earlier we have those conversations the better for the individual because leaving someone where they are performing poorly is cruel. It's wrong.'

Useful phrases

In this area of management, perhaps more than any other, communication is vital. I asked people whether there were any phrases they found useful when instigating difficult conversations. Some I have already quoted in the chapter but here they are again together with a few more:

- I have to deliver a fairly direct message to you and it is this…

- If I had been doing this I would want to be told so that I could improve.

- This is something I am guilty of doing/used to do.

- Presumably you are looking for feedback…

- I don't have evidence but it feels to me as if you are finding it hard to… what do you think?

Moving poor performers to different roles

One option for dealing with poor performers is to change their role. It is both a blessing and a curse that many areas of the public sector are so large that people can often be moved easily from job to job. The blessing is that it can be possible to find people roles that are better suited to their talents and interests or simply move them on to something new if they are stuck in a rut. 'Sometimes,' says Helen Bailey, 'good people need a new start elsewhere not because they have fouled up but just because they are getting boiled in treacle.' This treacle might be a particular manager with whom they don't gel, or a particularly intransigent project. The point is that a public sector manager will often have different job options at their disposal to try to get the best out of good people. Another advantage of moving people on within an organization is that it provides an easy opportunity to give slightly more straightforward feedback. 'In your new role you might want to pay more attention to...'

The curse is that it can be tempting to transfer staff in order to avoid a problem rather than dealing with it head on. And sometimes, it may even be rational for the manager if not for the organization to do so. The poor performer becomes somebody else's headache without you having to go through the hassle and awkwardness of confronting the issues. 'I palm off poor performers', admitted one interviewee. 'The wonderful thing about the civil service is that you can move people around fairly easily.' Avoiding dealing with poor performers in this way can be taken to even more extreme levels. 'Sometimes,' says consultant Stephen Taylor, 'the desire to move a couple of poor performers can become an excuse for an entire reorganization.'

So, as a manager, what can you do to ensure that the decisions to move people around made by you and the people who work for you are made for the right reasons? First of all, of course, it helps to have a robust appraisal process in place. If you are confident that appraisals genuinely reflect the performance of individuals, you can be much more confident that poor performers are being identified and managed effectively. Secondly, if you are being asked to approve a move, it is worth spending a considerable amount of time challenging the reasons for the move and, where possible, ensuring that the manager requesting the transfer of a member of staff has some stake in the success or otherwise of the move. Thirdly, if you yourself are moving the staff member on, it is worth asking whether this is something that is going to save you time and have the right impact on the remaining team members.

How Bloomberg moves people

Michael Bloomberg described a different approach to moving people around from his time at Bloomberg:

> One day when I was running my business I called my senior managers to a surprise meeting and said, 'Each of you is going to spend the next six weeks studying another department. You are not going back to your desks. I have somebody right now, cleaning them out and they will deliver the stuff in boxes to your new desk. For the next six weeks I want you to sit there and watch that agency and then tell me what they could do better. Who's going to run your department in the meantime? Your number two. And if you are going to sit here and tell me your number two can't do it, I'm going to dismiss you right now, because I've told you all along you have to have a number two who can fill in. I am going to find out whether they can.'
>
> Everybody was shocked initially but after six weeks they came back and said it was the most wonderful thing they had ever done and they were all ready to go back. And then the surprise was they all went back to jobs, but not in their original departments and not necessarily at the department they studied. Nobody quit and the company still does phenomenal business. That is harder to do in government because there are union rules and there are bigger differences between agencies but the concept of changing people around is a good one.

Firing poor performers

Many would say that in the public sector poor performance does not often enough lead to people losing their jobs. As seen in Chapter 2 on accountability, there are statistics which suggest that the public sector sacks fewer people than the private sector, although it is hard to compare like with like. There is certainly no practical reason why this should be the case. 'It is no harder to sack people in the public than the private sector', says Gill Rider. 'Employment law drives what you can and cannot do and it is the same for everyone.'

But three factors might make sacking people a less attractive option in the public sector. First of all, as already discussed, large public sector organizations often provide opportunities to move people to different roles rather than sack them.

Secondly, because it can be harder to measure the performance of an individual in the public sector it can often be harder to gather watertight evidence to illustrate poor performance. Without having clear evidence to justify such an extreme decision managers can feel inhibited, fearing lengthy bureaucracy and in some cases legal wrangles.

Thirdly, the public sector has less flexibility about pay-offs. The private sector has the discretion to offer generous settlements to people who are being asked to leave. Such settlements have the double benefit of making the manager feel less guilty and the person being dismissed less likely to contest the dismissal.

On top of all these elements are the challenges common to public and private sector managers: taking a job away from another human being is simply not a pleasant thing to do and usually involves significant emotional and bureaucratic effort. When you consider all these factors it is tempting to conclude that public sector managers can on occasion avoid firing people when they should. It is another example of an area in which it is easy to be lulled into not making a decision.

But other than flagrant errors or breaches of conduct, how can you know when it is right to fire someone rather than move them to a different role or develop them? I asked every single person I interviewed this question. Perhaps comfortingly, albeit unhelpfully, the universal response was 'I don't know'.

'Sometimes I've given people longer than I should have done because I thought they could make it', says Heather Rabbatts. 'Sometimes I've been told that I haven't given people long enough. I think you probably have to trust your instincts. Also, it's often easier to see when people are at the early stages of working for you. If you've been with them for a number of years you can get comfortable with their performance even if it isn't really acceptable.'

Ian Watmore finds it helpful to think about people using a frame-work made popular by Jack Welch, the former chief executive of General Electric:

> It is a simple two-by-two matrix where on one side you have achieving results for the organization and on the other living by the values of the organization. If you've got people who achieve the results and achieve the values, they are your superstars – you worship them, you fight to keep them. People who never get the results or know the values are also easy – you get rid of them. The hard two are the other two and Jack Welch said that the conclusion you get to relatively quickly in your management career is that you encourage and nurture the people who get the values but don't get the results because you've got good raw material.
>
> He said the hard ones and the ones that you deal with only after you've been an experienced leader are those that get the results but don't live the values. You have to fire those people and do so quite publicly because they are actually a huge drag on the rest of the organization. The whole organization would be given a lift disproportionately more than the loss of the results you would lose by that one individual going out of the door. And so I've spent quite a lot of my time thinking about that and concluded that in the end you do have to move those people on and if you don't move them on they corrode the whole organization and undermine what you're trying to achieve.
>
> I think that's probably my biggest lesson on performance management.

Many other people talked about the importance of people living the values. 'Sometimes there will be terrorists', said one manager. 'Well, if they're terrorists and they're sabotaging everything you're doing then they've just got to go.' But how do you identify whether people have the right values or attitude to be part of your team?

'You can just tell in a meeting whether somebody sees things the same way as you do', says Michael Bichard. 'And you can spot signs within the rest of the organization such as a lack of enthusiasm or the presence of sarcasm and cynicism. You very quickly suss out whether people are making an effort. You've got a lot of information which is coming in to you. Some of it is your observation, conversations you've had, but if somebody is going around slagging you off or slagging off the organization, it does get back to you. While it might be ill motivated in one or two cases, if it's coming back to you from different sources you begin to think that this person probably is saying these kinds of things. And then when you face them up with it, that normally is a bit of a shock because people don't like or don't expect to be faced up with those sorts of things. So you can normally tell whether someone is on side or not.'

And yet the advantages of not having to dismiss people are, of course, significant too. If you can keep people on board you don't disrupt the workplace, you don't lose institutional knowledge, you don't spend time and money recruiting someone new and, of course, if you can develop or move someone successfully then the organization will benefit as a whole.

So what conclusions can we draw? Perhaps the main conclusion is that there is no straightforward way of knowing when to fire someone. As a result, the decision to do so usually boils down to instinct. The clinching factor is less the quality of the job that somebody is performing but more the attitude and values with which they perform it.

Reflections on public v private attitudes to firing people

When he left the civil service in 1998, Robin Butler took on many advisory roles in the private sector, including as non-executive director at a FTSE 100 company. He has mixed views about the relative efficacy of the approaches both sectors take to dismissing people:

I was struck by how ruthless and unfair the commercial sector was by my standards... I think of a particular incident [at the FTSE 100 company] where they had to issue a profits warning after a computer project that went wrong. This in my view was the responsibility of the chap who ran that particular section. And we had a very good chief executive of the whole group, but the chairman said, 'It's not really going to be enough to satisfy the shareholders to get rid of the chap who ran the particular operation. The chief executive is going to have to go', and so the chief executive did go. He was an excellent fellow and doing an excellent job. This I felt wasn't fair, and I think the commercial sector does operate in an unfair way. It is not a way that is really open to the government sector, and I certainly always approach things by saying there's got to be a fair process. But I am not sure that that is the most effective way of doing things. Maybe sometimes the most effective thing is to say 'Well, life is unfair' and if people have lost confidence in you, it's not your fault, but that's life.

Recruitment

You've got to go into the job description and say, well, St Peter might have these attributes if he applies, but by and large we are not going to get everything, so what are the really important ones?   GEOFFREY DEAR

The final, and considerably more positive, section of this chapter considers recruitment. If you can get this right, you will not have to deal with poor performance.

Qualities to look for when recruiting

There is huge overlap between the qualities required in the private and public sectors. Among the most commonly mentioned by the people I interviewed were enthusiasm, curiosity and integrity, all of which apply in equal measure to both sectors.

'If they demonstrate enthusiasm for what they were doing previously,' says Paul Martin, 'then there is a good chance that they will carry this enthusiasm into their work for you. And the opposite is true if they don't.'

'Curiosity will help people spot what is going wrong and help them identify ways in which they could improve', says Chris Haskins.

For Michael Bloomberg the particular value of integrity lies in open communications. 'I'm looking for someone who will be straight with me if something is going wrong.'

But there are three further qualities which, although not unique requirements for people working in the public sector, can carry a greater weight there:

- **The ability to get along with people.** This may seem like a bland statement of the obvious. But it goes beyond the need simply to get along with your work colleagues. Most public sector workers will need to work with partners to get their job done. This might involve collaborating with agencies similar to your own to share intelligence or create efficiencies. Or it might involve collaborating with different agencies to solve complex problems – for example dealing with childhood obesity might require a combined effort between the local health provider, school and social services.

  In addition, public sector workers have much less discretion about whom they work with in the public sector. You are stuck with whichever politicians have been elected, you have to partner with whoever runs your local agencies rather than the neighbouring agency that you get on with better, and you have no choice about what type of customer you deal with. In these circumstances, it is important to hire people who are predisposed to be personable. 'I do rate personal skills very highly', says Ian Watmore. 'I worry not so much about what people say but about how they say it. If people are cocksure or overly aggressive or unnecessarily provocative or just stand there bluffing, I reckon that if I'm thinking it then lots of other people are going to be thinking that too. So I need to know that whoever works for me will represent me well and not put people's noses out of joint.'

- **The ability to take decisions.** Earlier chapters have talked about the understandable reluctance of public sector managers to take decisions. This stasis can come about either because it is often easier to do nothing or else pass a decision up to someone else in the food chain. So it is no wonder that many interviewees look for people who can talk convincingly about how they approach decision making (for example, how they delegate or escalate particular decisions) and are comfortable living with decisions that they have made in the past, even when they have been wrong.

- **A small ego.** Both Michael Bloomberg and Geoffrey Dear used exactly the same phrase to describe a quality they look for. They want people who 'have ambition, but not too much'. This may be another way of looking at the challenge of finding people with enough ambition to drive improvement, but not so much obvious personal ambition that they will alienate the people they must to work with, in particular the politicians. 'You need people who are comfortable in their own skin and have a low ego', says headhunter Stephen Bampfylde. 'Public sector managers need to work in an environment where they have responsibility for change but not absolute control.'

The process of selection

If you're going to base a decision on a job interview, you're mad. KEN LIVINGSTONE

When Ken Livingstone was looking for the right person to run the Olympic Development Authority, only one thing mattered: how closely the candidate's track record of achievement matched what was wanted. It was therefore an easy choice to pick David Higgins, 'not because he was a nice guy in the interview but because he had delivered the Sydney Olympics Village'.

Like Ken Livingstone, Gus O'Donnell is not a fan of the set-piece interview: 'So much of the skill of a public sector manager emerges in subtle ways which are hard to identify in the course of a short interview'. So, where possible, he will aim to see people in testing situations, for example briefing ministers or managing large meetings, to make an assessment about how well they can cope.

For Gill Rider, honest references were crucial and she took strong steps to ensure that they were done properly. 'I would check back after six months and if I felt that the references were wrong, and perhaps even wilfully misleading, I would raise it robustly with the referee.'

But if, like most organizations, the interview does form at least part of the process for selection, then below are some of the questions that the people I talked to used:

- What have you achieved? 'It's very important,' says Michael Bichard, 'particularly in the public sector to focus attention not on what people have done, or what posts they've held, but on what they've actually delivered when holding those posts.' There is certainly a risk that people will simply list what they have done rather than the outcome of what they have done. The obvious follow-up to this is: what difference did you personally make? Sometimes within the large structure of the public sector it can be easy to be a cog smoothly rotating around the machine and delivering projects without doing much more than anyone else competent within the role would have done.

- What do you like to do for fun? What makes you laugh? 'You are looking for someone that you will have to spend a lot of time with', says Stephen Bamfylde. 'You want to make sure that you will get along with them and enjoy their company.'

- What mistakes have you made? 'I always ask people a question that I could never answer the first time I was in an interview,' said one middle manager, 'which is: tell me about a mistake that you have made and what you learnt from it... I don't recruit people who are so egotistical that they have no idea what impact they and their mistakes have on other people.'

- Why do you want this job? Many use this (fairly obvious) question to test the motivation of the applicant. Are they genuinely interested in the area? Do they want to contribute to the team? Is it a stepping stone? Are they interested in the high-profile nature of the job?

- What is the hardest decision you have had to make? Geoffrey Dear says that this elicits useful responses as it illustrates not just what the candidate feels is important but also what sort of processes the candidate goes through under pressure.

- What is your approach to change? For Brian Dinsdale, delivering change is the hardest thing to achieve in an organization, and so finding out how a candidate has done this or would do this is revealing.

The headhunter's view – three ways of ensuring you get the wrong candidate

When public sector managers fail to pick the best candidate for a job it is usually for one or more of three reasons, says Stephen Bampfylde, who has been recruiting senior public sector managers for 25 years:

1 Interview by panel. 'Panels are a strange device to use for hiring people. They tend to militate against hiring extraordinary people in favour of the good average candidate who will offend the least number of people.'

2 Questions about the future instead of the past. 'I prefer my doctor to examine me before giving a diagnosis. Asking people to tell you how they would change an organization before they understand it gives too much weight to internal candidates and to dazzling talkers. It is far more useful to understand what they have done in the past.'

3 Too much process. 'We've got to a stage where, particularly for senior appointments, good candidates will be put off by having to fill in too many forms and the impression of bureaucracy it creates. Also the processes can get in the way of common sense – people can be concerned with ticking boxes rather than getting the right candidate. It comes from a good place of wanting to avoid nepotism and cronyism but it can go too far.'

Finally, here is the account of how Nick Walkley has adapted his approach to recruitment based on past experience:

> I've learnt that anybody who turns up to a director interview and says 'I know what I'm doing and I'm going to knuckle down and do it' should not be appointed. Because quite clearly if they think that's what's going to get them appointed, and that's what the job of a director actually is, then you're going to be in a whole heap of trouble, because they probably won't do either of those things.
>
> So now I'm really interested in people who have a cultural fit with this place, people who feel comfortable that you're not going to get an office, that your status is going to be determined as much by what you do as your pay grade. And I've been quite challenging in the interview about how they feel about this. So, I ask the question: 'We have an open plan work area, would you be comfortable with that?' They say 'Yes.' I say 'But there is no office and you have no PA.' And they say 'No, I'm absolutely fine with that.' So you then say immediately afterwards, 'So how would you go about organizing meetings with your management team?' The really smart ones respond 'Well, clearly I'd need to work to identify some resource and I'd need to figure out the best place to do these things.'

It is striking not just that Walkley realized that cultural fit was the most important ingredient for his recruits but that he also found practical ways of testing this potentially nebulous concept in his interviews.

Summary

It is challenging to give credible and honest appraisals, and more challenging still to be confident that the people below you in your organization are giving good appraisals to their direct reports.

There are a number of ways to improve the quality of appraisals:

- Gather information from as many sources as possible. This will give a more rounded view and the confidence to deliver difficult messages. These sources should include: performance data, systematically collected opinions from colleagues, partners and peers, and personal observation.

- Tie the appraisal objectives to the objectives of the organization rather than generic skill-sets.

- Demonstrate to the organization in your behaviour that you take appraisals seriously.

- Train people to deliver effective appraisals and to have straightforward conversations about performance.

Confront poor performance head on. Doing so will improve standards for everyone, it will save you time, it will probably be welcomed by other colleagues and the process may be less painful than you fear.

Sacking people is technically as easy in the public sector as in the private sector but it can often appear more difficult – the evidence of poor performance is less clear, people can be moved rather than sacked and the public sector does not have the flexibility of large pay-offs. There is no failsafe way of knowing when somebody should be fired rather than developed or moved. But it is harder to change the values of an individual than their skills.

Checklist

- Do you know what your three areas of personal development are and what you are doing to improve them? Do your staff know theirs?

- Do your staff value appraisals? Do you know how well appraisals are being delivered?

- Do your staff think that you value appraisals?

- Are you confident that appraisals are being honestly delivered? Do the write-ups of appraisals reflect the real opinions of the appraisers?

- Do your appraisal criteria reflect the goals of the organization/ department and what your customers value?

- Do you get enough input to appraisals from: performance data; colleagues; partners; peers?

- Have you seen your staff first hand in all types of situations that their jobs require?

- Do your staff feel that you deal with underperformance effectively?

Note

1 This has improved dramatically. By 2012, 90 per cent of staff received appraisals and a staff survey reported that 93 per cent of those who had received appraisals found them helpful.

Managing risk and innovation

06

> *The public sector can't give huge rewards when things go right but by goodness it can be brutal when things go wrong.*
> **ROBIN BUTLER**

Avoid risk like the plague. **MICHAEL HESELTINE**

Both risk and innovation are covered in this chapter. Although it would be stretching a point to suggest that they are two sides of the same coin, many of the inherent characteristics of the public sector – not least the low rewards and the brutal punishments alluded to by Robin Butler – can both encourage excessive risk aversion and stifle innovation.

This chapter begins with an overview of these characteristics and then suggests, first, ways in which risk can be managed appropriately, and second, ways in which you might encourage effective innovation.

Introduction – mitigating risk, stimulating innovation

When I interviewed Stephen Taylor, the experienced public sector consultant, he was not in a charitable mood: 'Getting the public sector to innovate is like teaching a man in a strait-jacket to dance.' The cause of this frustration (or at least part of it) was a meeting he had recently attended in a Whitehall department. At this meeting, a textbook test of the organization's attitude to innovation occurred: a new idea was put to them. 'It was a very interesting proposition,' says Taylor, 'which if it had been properly implemented would have had a huge benefit and saved a lot of money. And the first reaction of several people around the table was not how do we make this happen, but who will pay for it.' The excitement of the idea and the chances of it being implemented rapidly evaporated amid discussions about budgets, risks and governance.

Many academic studies explore approaches to risk and innovation in the public and private sector. They typically start with the premise that the public sector is more risk averse than it needs to be and not sufficiently innovative. My favourite is a statistical study which tests the hypothesis that because public sector jobs are more stable, they will attract more risk-averse people.[1] This study, like the others, is interesting but inevitably inconclusive. There are too many variables involved to make any meaningful comparisons. 'You want creativity, innovation and initiative in every organization,' Stephen Taylor observes, 'but that looks different in a nuclear power station to how it looks in an advertising agency.'

Certainly Gus O'Donnell would disagree with the premise that the public sector is naturally risk averse. 'What people don't realize is we are actually in some incredibly risky areas because we do things that no one else would dare to do. No private sector company would ever market a product, or sell a product where you had to make it available to everybody and do so for free. For example, delivering post to everywhere for the same price. Or offering health services for free. They'd just say, "You're mad, it's too risky."'

Geoff Mulgan, Chief Executive of the innovation foundation Nesta, defends the public sector's track record on innovation:[2] 'The caricature of public agencies as stagnant enemies of creativity is disproven by the innovation of thousands of public servants around the world who have discovered novel ways of combating AIDS, promoting fitness, educating, vaccinating vast populations or implementing new methods like intelligence-led policing or auctions for radio spectrum.' He also points out that arguably the greatest innovations of the past 50 years, the internet and the world wide web, both came from the public sector.

Characteristics that stimulate risk aversion and mitigate innovation

Despite these successes, there are pressures within the public sector which may militate against the ability of managers to manage risk appropriately and innovate.

Many of the things the public sector does are already inherently risky

David Normington does not look like a man carrying the cares of the world on his shoulders and yet when I met him he had one of the most stressful jobs in the civil service. As Permanent Secretary at the Home Office he was responsible for policing, terrorism and immigration. For him, risk comes not just from the significance of the work but also from the complexity and the scale of it. 'I carry seven or eight really big programmes on my top-level risk register – in any other organization you would stop four of them because it is too much risk to take on at once.' At the time, these programmes ranged from introducing ID cards to setting up a new points-based system for immigration. Why, therefore, doesn't he stop some of the projects? Partly because they need to be done and partly because the electoral timetable demands it – 'you have to have something to show the electorate'.

To add to the challenge, he was running a department which was, in his words, 'seriously beaten up' after John Reid infamously labelled it 'not fit for purpose' when he was Home Secretary. The challenge this presents is threefold: first of all, he needs to continue to deliver on a demanding programme of work with a poorly per-forming department, secondly, he needs to improve dramatically the performance of the department, and thirdly, he cannot afford to have any major public mistakes. 'I haven't talked much about innovation in the last three years', he says wryly.

Risks – and risk aversion – in the public sector are not limited to the Permanent Secretary in the Home Office. Wherever you look – education, planning, social services, health, police, armed forces –

public sector managers are taking responsibility for services which can dramatically affect people's lives. 'Risk aversion is not endemic because public sector managers are weak, hopeless, pathetic people', says Charles Clarke. 'It's actually because the costs of getting it wrong are so large.'

There can be a significant public penalty for making a mistake

In addition to the intrinsic importance of not making mistakes with public services, there is the potential for public exposure. 'We cannot afford to make too many mistakes,' says one manager 'because they get splashed all over the newspapers whereas similar mistakes in the private sector will go unnoticed externally.'

'If you try something new and it doesn't work,' says Michael Bloomberg, 'the word failure is in the headline, not the fact that you may have learnt a lot from the experience.'

Chris Haskins, like many before and since, tried to tackle the issue when he was in government. He was galvanized by what he perceived as the hysterical media coverage of the BSE outbreak in 1999. 'I suggested to Blair that I get the ministers and media together to discuss risk in government. I wrote to all the editors and none of them came and one of them responded by saying that he loved risk because it was what sold his newspapers. So we tried to see how you could manage risk sensibly in the public sector and the answer is you cannot.'

It is not just the media that creates this culture. It can also be driven by the adversarial nature of our political system at a national and a local level and the scrutiny that goes with it. Local authorities have scrutiny committees. At Westminster there are select committees. Both types of committee are independent and tend to be more interested in looking for examples of failure than success. 'Nobody stands back,' says Ian Watmore, 'and says "We tried 15 things, 12 went well, 2 were okayish and 1 went wrong." They focus on the one that went wrong and have an enquiry about it.'

The rewards for successful risk taking or innovation are not large enough

It is not just the downsides which can be inhibiting but the lack of an upside. For Jonathan Powell the lack of incentives for taking a risk is 'the single biggest problem in the civil service'. Certainly there are no significant financial rewards for public sector managers who take successful risks or implement terrific innovations. But the rewards for recognition are pretty low, too. Can you name the public servant responsible for the innovative Sure Start centres? Or the public servant who signs off the risks involved in letting thousands of drunk revellers into Edinburgh on New Year's Eve? To some extent this is because the politicians rightly take the praise (and sometimes the blame). In London the bicycle scheme is known as 'Boris bikes', named after the Mayor, Boris Johnson. My hunch is that his role in the scheme – albeit a hugely important one – was largely to champion it. Responsibility for the idea and the implementation most likely lies elsewhere.

This lack of recognition also stems from the fact that most significant public sector innovations or risks involve teams of people rather than individuals. Sure Start centres require collaboration between professionals in health, social care and education. Putting on a party in Edinburgh's town centre will involve the local authority, the police and the health service. In addition, it is very hard to pinpoint where ideas like Sure Start or 'Boris bikes' come from. More often than not they will emerge simultaneously from a number of different sources – think-tanks, universities, other countries – and then be developed over time.

So the penalties for failure are too large and the rewards for success too small. Here is an example of how these constraints can affect the way that problems are approached. In 1999, Chris Haskins was involved in the implementation of the minimum wage. The process of trying to anticipate every single scenario was, for Haskins, ridiculous:

> The civil servants were obsessed with having it absolutely waterproof. It was going to work. But the way they were going about it almost meant

that we would not have the minimum wage today. And I always remember one example of it they came up with was a case of a part-time 70-year-old newspaper boy in Stoke on Trent who would be worse off as a result – how would we cover this? Whereas I with [Tony] Blair was pressing for a slightly crude approach recognizing we would probably get 90 per cent effectiveness rather than 100 per cent. There are lots of people within Whitehall who recognize the absurdity but what it comes down to is that the intolerance of the scrutiny means that they are risk averse.

Managing risk effectively

Given these inherent, and entirely reasonable, constraints, how can you take a proportionate approach to risk management? Here are some ideas.

Start with the ubiquitous risk register

Whoever first came up with the idea of the risk register must be pleased with its progress. With the exception perhaps of accounting conventions it is hard to think of any management tool used as widely and as consistently. Every single interviewee talked about using a risk register as the basis for their approach to managing risk. These risk registers adhere to the same fundamental principles: you have a table which lists the risks, assesses their impact and likelihood, and sets out potential mitigations for these risks.

There are variations in format and terminology and occasionally in process. In the NHS, for example, there is widespread use of a five-by-five matrix which talks of consequence rather than impact and tightly defines how to rate these consequences for different types of risk. The emphasis here is on coming up with a numerically credible and standard way of categorizing risk.

There are also differences in how regularly different organizations review risks and how they respond to them. Charles Farr, the Director General of the Office for Security and Counter-Terrorism at the Home Office, is responsible for a risk register which, among other things, includes an assessment of the risks posed by terrorist attacks. But even for him, risk management begins with the bog-standard risk register: 'We have a pretty conventional approach... a list of risks with impact, likelihood and mitigating actions assigned to directors.' But, he adds, 'The difference in our case is that some risks can crop up unexpectedly – today for example we are bound up with managing the deportation of Abu Qatada which raises all sorts of risks for the government's reputation. Also, in some areas we examine risk particularly closely and it drives what we do perhaps more than other organizations. So the Olympic security programme and our resourcing and planning for it are heavily based on a very structured and detailed risk assessment.'

Maintaining a risk register is only one aspect of successful risk management and arguably a minor one. The culture and activities that lie behind it will play a greater role in determining how well an organization manages risk.

Set (and agree) the right expectations

Charles Farr believes that expectations around the risks associated with counter terrorism are very different in the United States and the United Kingdom. 'In the UK we have never promised to avoid any terrorist attack. Our aim is to reduce the threat so that people can go about their lives in an ordinary way. By contrast, in the [United] States and in some other countries departments and agencies are expected to eliminate threat and risk entirely. In the event of a terrorist attack heads may roll and it is very difficult for the agency most closely involved to avoid a public enquiry.'

If you are living with expectations around risk which are not deliverable, it can have a corrosive effect on your management processes, not to mention your emotional well-being. There are two elements to this: first of all, it is to set expectations that you can believe in yourself; secondly, it is to make sure that the key stakeholders around you – your colleagues, your bosses, the public – understand and agree with the expectations that are set. This is as relevant to managing counter-terrorism as it is to running an IT department.

There is a particular challenge in the public sector, which is the role that politicians play in setting public expectations. In Charles Farr's view, politicians have set the mood music and this explains the differences in approaches between the United States and the United Kingdom. 'American politicians have not accustomed their public to life with risk, whereas over the years it has been different here [the UK], going back to Irish terrorism.' In some instances, the politicians may have particular agendas to promote which will be dramatically at odds with the reality of what can actually be achieved, particularly if they are in opposition. So it is the task of the public sector manager, whether in transport, health, policing, planning, to do their best to ensure that politicians above all agree with the expectations being set around risk and will communicate them consistently.

Trust and be trusted

When Willie Whitelaw returned to the Home Office as Home Secretary again, Hayden Phillips observed a curious civil service phenomenon. The volume of paperwork fell. This happened, according to Phillips, because Whitelaw trusted his civil servants who in turn trusted him. 'We didn't feel the need to watch our backs and write up every meeting or decision in pedantic detail.'

Trust comes in a number of forms and is critical in a number of ways. Most of us will sense instinctively whom we trust and will absorb these instincts into the way we make our decisions. But it is rare to think about it in a systematic fashion. Which of your staff do you trust and which of them trust you? And what about your partners? Your colleagues? Your politicians? And your customers and citizens? And what is it about these different groups that you trust (or distrust) – their competence or their motivations? As with so many other areas, trust is especially important in the public sector. Services need to be delivered in partnership with people with whom you have no direct hierarchical relationship. Public servants will often be handling and sharing confidential data or information which would be damaging if leaked either deliberately or mistakenly. Citizens rely on the public sector to deliver highly important and personal services.

In all these situations, having a high degree of trust will make the processes easier and more effective and a low degree of trust will have the opposite effect. If an elderly person does not trust his local authority to deliver his meals on wheels on time then he is more likely to ring them up several times to confirm the time and to be unforgiving if the delivery is late. If a Treasury official does not trust a Home Office official with a particular report then she might make him come round to the Treasury to read it rather than send an electronic copy. If a local authority chief executive does not trust her local police and health partners to be able to deliver competently on a local safety or community project then she is unlikely to invest much of her own time and resources in making it happen.

Trust has a particular importance in managing risk. It is no coincidence that Charles Farr, who has some fairly extreme risks to manage, places huge emphasis on the importance of relationships. 'Trust underpins the entire risk management process from identifying and assessing the risk, to identifying mitigating actions to managing the risk itself if it materializes.' Trusting and being trusted at each of these stages will ensure integrity of process and an effective response.

So how do you build trust? Slowly and carefully. 'It is difficult to build and easy to destroy', a manager in one large public sector organization told me. 'I feel we have a culture of distrust in my organization and it filters down from the top. We have poorly defined and overlapping roles and often there isn't enough work to do, which means that people fight each other thinking it is a zero sum game. Also the flow of information from the top is poor, not just about performance or strategy. Sometimes people disappear from the organization without any explanation, so rumours start.' To build trust within her own team she did her best to ensure that there were no surprises, that she shared information with them, that she asked for her staff's opinions and that when people asked her to do something she did it or explained why she would not.

'Trusting your partners is tremendously important', another manager told me. 'One of the things I say to my staff is the more you can get out and get to know the people you deal with face to face the better. Fundamentally you need to have those personal contacts because it makes life a lot easier. You can build all the clever government systems you want but if people within that system don't like each other and don't trust each other, it isn't going to work.'

These actions – sharing information, doing what you say you will do, building relationships – are straightforward, at least to say, if not always to do. But perhaps the most helpful insight is to think of relationships in terms of trust and what impact they have on your ability to do a good job. Once you have identified the relationships where trust is most important and least present, you can invest time in them.

Values in counter-terrorism

Unsurprisingly perhaps, Charles Farr and his work have featured quite heavily in this chapter about risk management. I have included the set of values he has developed partly because they are unusually specific and interesting and partly because they emphasize the importance he places on relationships and knowledge in a role where managing risk is so central. The four values are:

- Know your subject. 'Become an expert because around you are other experts and if you don't have the expertise in your subject they won't listen to you.'

- Know your stakeholders. 'Stakeholders is such a hackneyed word but unless you really understand how organizations work and get inside their business and know what's worrying them, not just know their names and their telephone numbers, then you cannot do your job properly.'

- Know each other. 'Because in this area coordination is critical and can become a real problem unless you know and trust the people you are coordinating with.'

- Do it in the real world. 'I'm not interested in submissions unless they lead to change; we need to get over the idea that paperwork is a success. It's not – it's just a means to an end.'

These values drive the behaviour of his staff in practical ways. 'So if you want to go off to Pakistan for a week with no specific objective other than to learn more about your subject area or your stakeholders, I will fund and support that.'

Constantly use your personal Geiger counter

The formal processes and discussions around risk need to be supplemented informally. When John Browne was Chief Executive at BP he would always take opportunities to assess risk. 'Good managers don't say: "Right, now we're going to have a day on risk and then we're not going to talk about it again." But every time you meet anybody you ask: "How's it going? What's on your mind? What are your risk issues?" You have to live it and then the systems should take care of the reporting.'

Paul Roberts thinks about managing risk by running a personal Geiger counter to pick up danger signs:

> All the time I'm trying to measure fragility in the organization. It means that I put a lot of energy into just trying to touch base with people all the time. I'm consciously looking for signs of loss of confidence or uncertainty to detect when an organization is either doing too much or is too close to the edge... where I think the organization is doing too much, because I think all organizations go through periods like this, I then find ways of applying the brakes and I deliberately pull back on initiatives to try and restabilize.

Of course, most managers will instinctively do much of this. But what I like about the approach Roberts outlines is that it is very conscious. By asking himself the question – how fragile is the organization? – he is explicitly forcing himself to think about, and potentially act upon, emerging risks in a more proactive manner.

Keep it simple – principles not process

Many interviewees talked in terms of keeping risk management simple. In practical terms this means two things: a short risk register and a clear set of principles which help people know how to behave at all times.

When Geoffrey Dear took over at the West Midlands Police he found that they had Standing Orders – the manual which set out codes of behaviour – which ran to 1,300 pages. He immediately empowered one of his brightest officers to boil these down to a number of key principles (it had to be fewer than 10 in case they became known as the 10 commandments). Dear himself put the first in place, which was that every officer will be judged on the honesty of the decision he or she makes at the time, even if later it is proved wrong. This clarity made him more comfortable that risks were being managed effectively than 1,300 pages of process, though coming up with the principles was only the start. 'Once we had put it together we had to demonstrate in the months that followed that we really meant it and so this meant saying in public that we got this wrong but that I would not castigate officers provided they had adhered to the principles. Morale and efficiency went up sky high and we won more respect from the media and the public.'

A strong narrative of the type discussed in Chapter 2 on accountability can also play the same role. 'The only way to deal with risk,' says Charles Clarke, 'is through strong leadership and a strong narrative and direction so that you can see how a particular course of action fits. People will be tolerant of mistakes and more likely to take reasonable risks.'

Sometimes it takes a certain type of character and personality to take and handle risks. Helen Bailey, the former Chief Executive of Islington Borough Council, is a case in point. Bailey is an immediately bold, charming and charismatic presence. When we met she reeled off a number of risks she had taken during her career. At Islington, every time Arsenal won a big trophy they would seek her permission to hold an open-top parade through the borough. The police were invariably cautious and told her that she would be held responsible for any problems. And she would give permission 'and I'd walk up the road during the parade crossing my fingers and wondering whether I should go on past the police station or just book myself a cell right now to save them all the work later'.

In another instance she ignored what she was told were statutory requirements which would have stopped the council renting building space jointly with the local Primary Care Trust. Sharing the space was an obviously sensible thing to do but placed her and Islington at some potential legal and financial risk. In both cases she was directly taking responsibility on her shoulders for situations which could unravel very publicly and very damagingly.

Why did she feel capable of taking such risks? 'Because often the risks that people are alerting you to are risks that have potentially serious consequences but actually no likelihood of happening.' That may well be true but I also think that, like many successful leaders, she has the temperament to live with risks like these and take the decisions that expose her to these risks. Not everyone is built this way and it is worth asking whether you and your managers have the character to live with the risk taking required for the role.

Innovation – or the lack of it

On the face of it, innovation and how to stimulate it is a more glamorous topic than managing risk. Indeed, public sector managers can get help on innovation in a number of places. There are innovation consultancies, there are non-profit organizations set up specifically to promote innovation, such as Nesta or the Young Foundation, and there are any number of books or research available with ideas for making your organization more innovative. The public sector also develops its own internal resources. For example, the NHS used to have an Institute for Innovation and Improvement and the Department for Business, Innovation and Skills (BIS) had a team (and website) devoted to public sector innovation.

But if the people I spoke to are any guide, these resources rarely get used by senior managers. Not one of the interviewees said that they had actively sought to make their organization more innovative. And not one, when asked how to increase innovation, mentioned a methodology or activity of the sort that innovation consultants would promote. They would invariably say that they were keen on innovation and would encourage it when it occurred, but they did not say that they would invest much time or money generating these innovations, nor were they easily able to point to innovations that had emerged from any recognizable innovation process. 'I think most innovation is tosh', says Nick Walkley. 'Most people who claim to be innovators should get a proper job. And most authorities desperately peddling some innovative process really ought to think about what it is they should be doing. The problem with innovation in the public sector is that what it actually means is the generation of some boutique project to satisfy a particular management team. What it rarely means is the use of creative processes to change the direction of mainstream service delivery.'

What conclusions can we draw from this? Is it silly to think of innovation as a concept in its own right? Should new ideas just emerge from other management activities without having to focus on 'being creative'? Or are managers, even very successful managers, missing a trick by not focusing on innovation?

Geoff Mulgan, the Chief Executive of Nesta, is not sympathetic. 'Managers talk about innovation and like to think of themselves as innovative. But they don't take it seriously. They have no knowledge of the methods, no way of thinking about how much they should spend on it, organize it, assess if they're doing it well or badly; and they have no examples to draw on... this has to change.'

Simon Tucker, who succeeded Mulgan as Chief Executive of the Young Foundation, is similarly downbeat. 'There have been some big top-line initiatives about innovation but these are not matched by any serious purpose. There is not a strong enough belief that they will work.' In his view, these initiatives are often undermined by half-hearted staffing – 'you usually get people who are too junior to really shift an organization' – and the same old routines. 'I don't think I've ever been at a workshop which has generated a good idea,' he reflects ruefully. In Tucker's view, radical innovation – as opposed to the incremental improvements achieved by improving processes – requires different skill-sets. 'You need to skill up staff for innovation in the same way as you train staff to manage budgets.' As a rough guide, he recommends that organizations should invest at least 1 per cent of their budget in innovation.

How to encourage innovation

Even if the interviewees did not follow the advice of Mulgan and Tucker, they did have some experiences around innovation to share.

Look outside

The obvious source for new ideas is to look to other people and other organizations. This might be as simple as inviting interesting people to come in and speak to staff, particularly people who have had success in other sectors. Paul Roberts stimulated new ideas by asking outsiders to take a look at what was going on. 'I would pay experienced people to come in for a few days and say: "You can go anywhere, you can do anything you like, and I want you to give us a sense of where we are. Are we doing the right things? Are we being creative enough?" I'm very keen to find ways of looking at organizations which are not about inspection, because inspection just drives you into a defensive, uncreative mode.'

Michael Bloomberg goes further and actively seeks to bring different people onto his staff. 'The problem with any organizations that don't bring in new people is that they don't innovate and adopt technologies. In government it is hard to do because generally there isn't a lot of turnaround.' He cites his Commissioner for Public Transportation as an example of the benefits of bringing in someone new. Her background was as a transportation consultant, not a civil servant. She has galvanized the department. 'She has brought a whole new approach. A whole new group of ideas. She has done a dozen things... none of which the old person would have ever done. The old person's job was running the agency and she did it really well for five and a half years. The new person's job was coming up with new things. She has got 10 crazy ideas every day and some of them are really good.' One such idea was to shut down Park Avenue for a day and turn it into a pedestrian zone. 'It is a great idea and has been a huge success', says Bloomberg. 'I would never have come up with it in a million years.'

And then there are other organizations. As mentioned before, the public sector has a tremendous advantage: there are large numbers of organizations doing similar things and no competitive barrier to stop them sharing their latest ideas with each other. There are many mechanisms for exploiting this advantage. They range from more formal mechanisms such as mutual inspections and best-practice-sharing boards to more informal conferences and meetings. And sometimes a specific situation will prompt managers to exploit this resource. 'At my last prison,' said Helen Carter, 'we had problems with violence with the young offenders so we went and looked at a number of other establishments and said: "How have you managed to reduce this?" And we didn't actually take the model from any one prison that we saw because we didn't think that any of them fitted. But what we did do was take individual elements which we thought would work for us.'

How one meeting catalysed a new approach to treating cancer

In April 2012, University College London Hospital opened its new Cancer Centre. It took 10 years to come to fruition and cost £100m. It is unlike any other cancer centre in the UK, from its award-winning Hopkins-designed building to its state-of-the-art medical equipment. As a medical facility the major innovation is its emphasis on maintaining the independence of patients, for example by enabling them to self-medicate in many instances. The result is a better quality of life for cancer patients and fewer expensive overnight hospital stays during treatment.

So how did this major innovation come about? Through a contact and a meeting. Robert Naylor, the Chief Executive of UCLH, explains:

I knew the chief executive of the Sloane-Kettering hospital in New York which was one of the best cancer hospitals in the world. He invited me to visit and while I was there he showed me his new ambulatory cancer centre. Effectively they had bought a hotel block and kept half as a hotel and changed the other into a cancer centre. The whole philosophy was that they were focused on the patient's quality of life. We compared case-notes and reckoned that 35 per cent of our patients wouldn't get anywhere near being an inpatient under their system because they would be treated in this different way. And the other thing was that each floor in their centre specialized in a different form of cancer.

I remember coming back on the plane and thinking what would I do if a member of my family was diagnosed with cancer, would I spend lots

*of money and get on a plane with them to Sloane-Kettering or would
I stay in the UK? And the answer is that it would have been a very
difficult choice to make. So rather than sending people to America
I thought we should create something similar in the UK. And that was
nearly 10 years ago.*

*The inspiration for this was almost entirely down to that single visit and
my understanding that this was a really important thing to do.*

Look inside

But there are also ways of looking within your own organization.
'What works best,' says Nick Walkley, 'is bringing frontline staff face
to face with end users, full stop. That tends to be the most creative
process. So in customer services we just invite a group of our customers
to come and talk to the people who serve them. It tends to generate
thoughts and ideas right at the frontline.'

At Westminster Council, Peter Rogers and the leader Sir Simon
Milton attempted to generate good ideas via a sizeable reward
scheme. They selected an employee of the month and employee of the
year award schemes worth £1,000 and £12,000 to encourage people
to come forward with their innovative achievements. 'It was also,'
says Rogers, 'a great way of star-spotting people who had done something that wasn't in their job description but could be easily incorporated in excellent practice. And it helped set a culture for innovation.'
Less formally but just as effectively, they would visit different departments together each month to find out what was going on. Although
in some instances this allowed Rogers and Milton to sniff out problems,
in the majority of cases this gave managers a chance to show off
about the services they were providing and ask for support to make
changes. 'There is nothing better than learning how to improve something from somebody who knows the job and knows how to do it.'

Internal innovation can be encouraged further by making sure that
the good ideas get acted on and celebrated. Michael Bloomberg oozed
this can-do attitude when he talked about ideas within New York.
Here he is describing one such idea:

One of the chancellors of the school system comes up with the idea of parent coordinators. We have 1,400 people, one for each school, who have a cell phone. We give the cell phone number to all the parents. Then if they have got a question, if they want to talk to the teacher or if the teacher wants to tell the parent this kid hasn't had a bath or didn't do his homework or is putting the girl's pigtail in the ink well, it is the parent coordinator who can make or take that call. Great idea. I was annoyed with it because it is so damn obvious and I never thought of it.

Both the excited tone of his language when talking about it as well as the fact that he implemented the idea must be very motivating in an environment in which failure so often gets more coverage. 'The NAO's [National Audit Office] review of successful IT projects I would say is a document that hasn't got an enormous readership alas, nor does it get much media coverage', reflects Gus O'Donnell ruefully. 'The media is much more likely to report on our failures than our successes so we need to encourage risk taking and innovation by celebrating successes.'

Innovation for Permanent Secretaries

Ian Watmore describes how a small, cost-free innovation made by Gus O'Donnell 'turned the Permanent Secretaries from a bunch of talented individuals into a team'. Permanent Secretaries meet weekly. These meetings used to follow conventional agendas, with individual departments reporting back on particular issues. This format could create an environment in which people were either uninterested or confrontational. O'Donnell's innovation was to encourage individual permanent secretaries to lead discussions on issues that were specific to their own department (eg the Permanent Secretary at the Home Office to lead a discussion about immigration) and ask their colleagues for help and advice. For Watmore, this small tweaking of the format has helped transform the way Permanent Secretaries work together: 'He turned it [the meeting] from people making witty and intellectually sharp comments across the table about each topic to working together on solving a common issue.'

Remember to innovate in the good times, not just the bad

A final reflection on innovation. Often the drive to innovate comes from moments of pressure. No crisis, as the mantra has it, should go to waste. From such crises – whether financial or environmental – innoations may emerge in the form of processes, products or structures.

But managers should not just rely on a burning platform to force innovation. In fact, in many ways it is the moments of relative calm in which it can be easier to try new things. Over the past 20 years, Gateshead Council has taken huge risks and been extraordinarily innovative. In an area with pockets of extreme deprivation it has raised and spent more than £500m delivering cultural projects such as the Baltic Centre for Contemporary Art, the Sage Gateshead music centre, the millennium bridge and, perhaps most imaginatively and daringly of all, Anthony Gormley's Angel of the North. To many it was not at all clear why a relatively poor north-eastern city should invest so much time and money in a series of arts projects when it could be getting more tangibly useful things for its money, like better community centres or more social workers. And yet not only did they take these decisions – and the flak that they knew would go with them – but now they are widely perceived to be huge successes. How were they able to do this?

Jan Parkinson, who was Director of HR, attributes this to stability and success. 'You can take risks and be innovative when you're in a position of strength... The leader and chief executive at the time were a partnership of 17 or 18 years' standing. It was a very stable council and it was also a council that was delivering on the basics. It was improving educational resources year on year. It was safe in terms of its social services and it was popular with electors so it was a good time to take risks.' So, by all means take advantage of the crises, but also be proactive in taking advantage of the good times to try out new things.

Summary

The public penalties for failure and the small rewards for success mean that the incentive to take risks or innovate in the public sector is low.

To help manage risk appropriately:

- Use a risk register as a starting point, but only as a starting point.
- Set and agree expectations with all stakeholders and, where appropriate, ensure that your politicians communicate these expectations to the public.
- Assess the levels of trust you have between key stakeholders and maintain or increase them as needed.
- And: use informal ways of assessing risk to supplement formal approaches; have a strong narrative; keep it simple.

Despite the enormous amount of resources and methodologies available, very few public sector managers actively promote innovation within their organizations because they do not see the value of treating innovation as an area of focus in its own right.

Instead managers should innovate by:

- looking outside their organization by bringing outsiders in to speak, advise or work or by spending time with peer groups;
- looking inside by creating a culture of innovation which is open to implementing new ideas and celebrating successful innovations;
- bringing staff face to face with end users;
- trying new things when they are in a position of strength.

Checklist

On risk:

- Do you have a risk register? To what extent does it drive behaviour?

- Do all key stakeholders (internal and external) share the same view of individual risks?

- How much do you trust your stakeholders? How much do they trust you?

- What impact do these levels of trust have on your effectiveness?

- Are you thinking about how to build levels of trust?

- Do you have a sense of how much pressure your key members of staff are under? And how fragile your organization and team are generally?

On innovation:

- Do you actively think about how to innovate?

- Do your staff think they work in an innovative organization?

- How do you encourage your staff to come up with new ideas?

- How do you bring new ideas into your organization?

- What sources do you have for finding out about new ideas in your peer organizations? How good are they and how often do you take advantage of them?

Notes

1 Barry Bozeman and Gordon Kingsley, Risk culture in public and private organizations, *Public Administration Review*, 58 (2), 1998, pp 109–19.

2 Geoff Mulgan, *Ready or not? Taking innovation in the public sector seriously*. Nesta Provocation 03 (Nesta, London, 2007).

Managing decision making

07

"With important decisions if you have actually analysed the problem, and the history, and know the issues inside out then the answer is usually obvious. **KEN LIVINGSTONE**

There are very few decisions that are 100 per cent – we pay people in the public sector for decision making under uncertainty. **GUS O'DONNELL**

This chapter tackles the broad topic of decision making. How do you make good decisions? How do you know when you have got it right and when you have got it wrong? What processes should you go through before making a decision?

Introduction – public sector decision making

Decision making is part of everyone's professional and personal life. But there are a number of elements which, if not unique to decision making in the public sector, at least add some nuance. Perhaps the most significant is the difficulty of making any decision at all. 'It is psychologically attractive not to take decisions', says Charles Clarke. 'Decisions in the public sector are so much more exposed than decisions in the private sector. The ability of relatively low-level sector managers to take responsibility for what they've done is very difficult because it gets passed back up the line to the chief officer or then to the elected officials and people find it very, very difficult to let go in those circumstances.'

There are other reasons why it can be hard to make decisions in the public sector, which have been dwelt on in previous chapters. The need to build consensus, for example between different public bodies who share responsibility for delivery. The need to build consensus, too, between managers holding the budgets and the frontline professionals providing the services. And perhaps above all, the sheer complexity and consequences of so many of the decisions that public sector managers make.

How to improve your decision making

Although this chapter cannot promise the clarity that Ken Livingstone brings to his decision making, it can offer some thoughts about how to approach these challenges.

Just make decisions – and encourage others to do so

It is hard to argue with the proposition that managers should be good at making decisions. But how can you overcome the 'psychological attraction' of not taking decisions?

- **Assess the impact of not making a decision.** 'Often the consequence of not taking a decision is worse than the consequence of taking a decision', says Charles Clarke. His former boss, Tony Blair, used this logic to urge the world to intervene in Libya using similar language: 'Inaction is also a decision, a policy with consequence', he wrote in *The Times* in March 2010. Although few managers will face quite such dramatic decisions, this logic applies equally to other areas. These might include decisions around spending money on a project or dealing with a tricky personnel issue. A particular challenge, according to Peter Rogers, is to take the decision to shut something down. 'There is,' he says, 'a time when you pull the plug on things that are bad investments and I think that takes some courage, particularly if it's something that matters to the organization,'

- **Remember that making a decision may be more important than the decision itself.** 'Nine times out of ten it really doesn't matter what decision you make', says Heather Rabbatts. 'Just make it.' Stephen Taylor describes working with a local authority chief executive who was agonizing about restructuring her senior management team. She was second guessing how the organization would respond and how individuals would respond, and would keep going back to the drawing board. 'I suggested that she should just declare what she was going to do and just do it. And she did and it worked a treat. The people who didn't like it tolerated it and the people who did like it thrived, and it meant she didn't struggle for 18 months with people she didn't really want and she removed uncertainty from the organization.'

- **Take comfort in the process you have gone through to reach the decision.** Provided that you can demonstrate to others that you spoke to the right people and looked at the right evidence, it will be hard for others to find fault with what you have done. It is acceptable to make an honest mistake or to interpret things differently. It is less acceptable to have ignored obvious inputs to the decision.

These three elements are important not just to help you make your own decisions but also for those working for you who make decisions. 'If you have more decision makers, you can have more decisions', says Bloomberg. Part of this is being clear with them about what they are responsible for, and part of it – perhaps the harder part – is making sure they feel that responsibility. 'Do not,' warns Stephen Taylor, 'allow your staff to "run things by you".'

Make the effort to get good data

" *In God we trust; all others must bring data.*
WILLIAM DEMING, AMERICAN STATISTICIAN

Obviously, getting the right data to enable you to make decisions is important. But how much time should you spend gathering data? And what should you do if the quality of the data is poor?

As a management consultant I spent a considerable amount of time gathering and analysing data in order to help public sector bodies make decisions. This could be a frustrating process. The data would be incomplete or inconsistent and sometimes would be impossible to find altogether. Often we would end up settling for second-rate data because we did not have enough time or money to do more. This made it much harder to decide what to do and, crucially, much harder to persuade people about what should be done. You are not likely to take difficult decisions to cut or invest or share or merge unless you feel reasonably sure about the data. Nor are you likely to bring with you people who are antagonistic because they will be able to pick holes in your conclusions.

Merrick Cockell has been Leader of the Royal Borough of Kensington and Chelsea since 2000. He and his counterparts at the London Borough of Hammersmith and Fulham and at Westminster City Council – all Conservative-led authorities – have decided to join up their services in a number of key areas. This is a genuinely and unusually radical course of action driven by a desire to be more efficient. How good was the data on which they based this decision? Not that good to start with, from the sound of it. 'Many data comparisons are guff,' says Cockell, 'they don't compare like with like. Only by going into the tri-borough arrangement have we been able to surface real comparisons. Doing it together means that there is nowhere to hide.'

This data analysis has enabled them to compare costs and quality across their services in order to decide how they should be managed. For example, according to Cockell, the data showed that Kensington and Chelsea's in-house IT service was more cost-effective and responsive (in some areas) than the outsourced IT services being delivered by the other two boroughs. This is a good example of the power of data. The instinct of many Conservative politicians would probably be to assume that the private sector would deliver more efficient services. In this instance, robust data which they trusted suggested otherwise for some services.

Robin Wales, Mayor of Newham, is a data enthusiast. 'The weakness in public policy is that our research is woeful and our evidence base is extremely poor.' His first point of call on any decision is to seek out the data. 'If a council tenant says to me in my surgery that their housing conditions are not very good, I will get a survey done to find out what other people tell us. If the survey confirms what I'm hearing then I'm comfortable doing something, but if what I'm hearing contradicts it then we'll do more research. Of course, we don't need to be perfect and some margins of error are fine, but we do need to do a lot more generally than we currently do.'

Michael Heseltine is slavishly devoted to collecting data in the cause of good decision making. 'It is one of my theories that you have to get into the detail and challenge it', says Heseltine. 'It doesn't matter so much when you just have 50 guys with quill pens and you can see them, but when you have 169,000 as I had at the Ministry of Defence then it's vital.' He lived up to this theory. He was instrumental in setting up the Audit Commission and also developed the Management Information System for Ministers (MINIS) which broke down costs and tasks in his department with a level of granularity not seen before in Whitehall. He is also a huge fan of organograms. Every new department he entered, he would ask for organograms. Very often they would not have them, which in his view was telling in itself. But once he received the organograms he would pore through them, looking for oddities 'where one answered to one answered to one' and getting a feel for the size and shape of the organization.

One anecdote gives a particularly good insight into the lengths he would go to find data. When he became Secretary of State at the Department of the Environment in 1979 he was part of a government committed to reducing public expenditure and the size of the civil service:

> I told them that no job could be filled without my agreement. We employed 52,000, so this was quite a thing. So they would come to tell the secretary of state we need some plumbers, and I would ask 'Why do you need plumbers?' and we would talk about it. I ran that system for six months, and after six months I discovered that for every ten requests we actually needed to recruit six. So I put in place an annualized reduction of 40 per cent [for new hires] for the next three years, which helped us take 13,000 people out of the department.

Getting the data gave Heseltine the confidence to make this decision and see it through.

Michael Barber knows a thing or two about collecting data. In his role as founder and head of the Prime Minister's Delivery Unit he spent much of his time cajoling central government departments into providing data that could be used to analyse and improve performance:

> Most people would agree that you need good data but then they say it will be too difficult and expensive to collect. Too often people have just given up. But there is absolutely no excuse for not having data. That's especially true now that data in all kinds of ways is cheaper and easier to collect than it was even 10 years ago. And the amount the data cost is so small for the amount of running the services and the improvements you want to make. Once you actually think it through the costs are trivial.
>
> People will also tell you that the data doesn't tell you everything you need to know. That's all true, but it's not an argument for not having any. I think it's central to public sector management, particularly when people are managing for productivity outcomes with restricted costs. Without data you just cannot do that.

So how did he go about collecting data? 'Through sheer bloody-mindedness, just persisting until they do it. And what we found – and I've found this all around the world now – is the first reaction to suggesting people need better data is exactly the list of excuses that you would expect. But when they've got the data, they love it, because suddenly they can do their job.'

Get first-hand information

But on its own, data may not be enough. 'Robert Macnamara [the US Secretary of Defence] made appalling decisions in Vietnam,' says Charles Guthrie, 'because he didn't really talk to people on the ground but relied on technical intelligence. I suspect this was because his background was in manufacturing on a super scale at General Motors. So using his numbers he came up with clever ways of using electronic warfare and inflicting the greatest amount of damage in the most efficient way. It was all very well saturating the jungle with agent orange or carpet bombing, but every time this happened he probably recruited another thousand people to the Viet Cong and extended the conflict. Of course you need the numbers and analysis but you have got to get out and talk to people to be truly effective. You have to do both.'

Guthrie is not alone in advocating the importance of getting this first hand information. 'You never have as much time as you should do for everything,' says Geoffrey Dear, 'but the one thing I was ruthless about was getting out to the sharp end. I always made sure that I had a day out inside the force once a week and if I missed it I had two days on another week.'

For Dear, and many others, this serves a number of purposes. You get to see first hand the issues your staff are dealing with, you have the chance of getting to know frontline staff, and for very senior managers like Dear it is a chance to cross-check the information your direct reports are giving you. Here is Dear's description of how it worked for him:

I always announced where I was going so that there was no suggestion that the boss is creeping around in the shadows trying to catch us out. They knew I was going there and I wouldn't just do visits between nine to five. It is very important in that environment to be up at 2 am just occasionally. It does wonders because you may not have contributed very much but actually they have seen you there and you cared and they knew you knew what it was like. And I would always have a good chat. How is it going? Tell me about the new system, the new equipment. That sort of thing. And if they told me something wasn't working I would take action to make sure it did. Of course, it also makes everyone underneath you, the middle managers, do the same thing. So it paid massive dividends in morale and standards.

John Monks, too, is a huge advocate of getting out and about the shop floor:

I did a day and a half a week and it was the best thing that I ever did. It gave me a lot of confidence in the top-level decisions we were making to know that I had my feet in the provinces as well... it gave me lots of anecdotes to use, to make a point. So when trade union leaders said that their priority was to change the labour laws back to the era before Mrs Thatcher, I knew that wasn't true. I had been in different workplaces and they were talking about investment in the future and training opportunities, not about strike laws.

For both Monks and Dear, spending time getting first-hand information was something they incorporated naturally into their jobs and it would generally inform their decision making. In other instances, making the effort to get this information can be prompted by a specific issue. In the early 1980s significant racial tensions culminated in riots in Brixton and Toxteth. Hayden Phillips was tasked with working out what could be done. He took the step – unusual at the time – of going round the country asking minority groups how they felt they were being treated. 'This enabled me to write an unconventional civil service report full of real-life anecdotes which gave it huge credibility and made it stick out from the crowd.' It is interesting that, as for Monks, much of the value for Phillips came from the stories that he was able to glean from his experiences and their usefulness in communicating what he wanted to report to others.

Of course, most managers recognize that seeing things first hand can be useful. But it is easy for these sorts of visits to become subordinate to the hurly-burly of the closer-at-hand demands and deadlines of working in an office. The challenge is to make the time and, as Michael Bichard did for his staff at the Department for Education, make it legitimate for your staff to make the time, too.

Of course, gathering first-hand information has another benefit, particularly for public sector workers. Witnessing the issues that you are trying to solve can be very motivating. As described in Chapter 2, Kevan Collins, the former Chief Executive of Tower Hamlets, spent huge amounts of time with his frontline staff in the *Undercover Boss* programme to try to learn more about his organization. His reflections at the end of the programme capture the benefits of getting this first-hand experience: 'It's so important in life to feel that there's a kind of moral purpose about what you do. And I think this has just given it another shot. I'm going back [to the chief executive role] with a new energy. I'm going back with new knowledge and I'm going back with a renewed appreciation, I think, of why I do what I do.'

Seek independent expertise

As well as getting first-hand information from sources connected to your organization, it can be helpful to find independent sources. 'A leader should have independently acquired understanding of the areas he oversees',[1] writes Rudolph Giuliani. Giuliani is at pains to say that this is not so that he can second guess and do the jobs of his expert staff for them. It is more that he can have enough knowledge to understand what he is being told and challenge where appropriate. To get this expertise, Giuliani reads everything he can find on subjects relevant to his workplace and talks to independent experts where he can find them.

Jonathan Powell took this approach during the panic of the foot and mouth outbreak in 2001 where he made a conscious effort to break out of the Whitehall bubble and find a different perspective. 'To try and keep a grip on reality, I maintained contact with a farmer in Cumbria whom Tony had met on a visit there. I phoned him most days to get a farmer's-eye view of the problem.'[2]

Independent expertise can be particularly useful when challenging your own experts. Brian Dinsdale sought independent advice to help him during an incident in his time as chief executive at one council. The council looked after six very disabled people whose care was costing £1m per year. He wanted to build a facility which would look after all of them centrally and would cost £600,000 per year. 'I was being told by the social workers that this is totally impossible. You can't do it. All these people need individual care.' In order to move forward, Dinsdale had to get external advice from social workers elsewhere that his proposal would not reduce quality to unacceptable levels. He then had to advise elected members to take the decision in the wider interests of the council and hope it didn't blow up in his face. The independent advice he got both gave him the confidence that his instincts were right and gave him evidence to demonstrate this to others, particularly the politicians.

Of course, it can also be valuable to challenge others to get the independent expertise that they need. Michael Barber recounts the following exchange with the Department of Transport (DOT) during at his time at the Prime Minister's Delivery Unit (PMDU):

PMDU: We've noticed this huge dip in the reliability of the railways in the autumn.

DOT: But surely you've heard about leaves on the line?

PMDU: Yes, we've heard about leaves on the line. What are you going to do about it?

DOT: What can we do? Autumn comes every year.

PMDU: We know autumn happens every year. Why does it take you by surprise?

DOT: Well, what would a plan for autumn look like?

PMDU: Is there any other country in the world where the leaves fall off the trees in the autumn?

DOT: Yes.

PMDU: But what about any other country where the leaves fall off the trees in the autumn and the railway performance is consistently good in the autumn?

'So they started looking around,' says Barber, 'and they came up with Canada. But there they cut all the trees down near the railway, so that's cheating. And then they came up with Poland. And Poland has a system. So then we adopt the Polish system and we deal with the leaves on the line problem.'

Although it is tempting to mock the attitude of the Department of Transport, Barber draws a more general lesson. 'I think they [the civil service] are good, competent people. But I think professional people – certainly not just civil servants – need regular challenge.' Seeking independent expertise is one way of bringing this challenge to bear.

Identify your big picture(s)

In his speech to the Conservative Party Conference in 2008 David Cameron revealed his big picture: 'Every big decision, every big judgement I make: I ask myself some simple questions. Does this encourage responsibility and discourage irresponsibility? Does this make us a more or less responsible society?'

It is useful to have some sort of framework to determine decision making. Without such a framework, decisions can be reactive and inconsistent. With it, they can be for a purpose. Three types of big picture came up during the interviews.

The first is the strategic big picture of the sort outlined by Cameron – what is the grand desired outcome? The outcome that Cameron seeks is a responsible society. This is a formula that politicians often like. In opposition, Cameron apparently used to ask his shadow business secretary Ken Clarke just one question about any proposal he came up with – will this lead to growth? Nick Clegg's equivalent is to ask whether it will create a fairer society.

A good example of a manager setting this sort of question comes from Ian Blair, the former Commissioner of the Metropolitan Police. In his autobiography he writes: 'I asked my senior colleagues to think of a test for themselves: when a friend's house was burgled in a part of the Met in which they did not work, were they perfectly content that the matter would be dealt with well or would they ring someone senior they knew there just to make sure that an eye was cast over what had been done?' In this one simple question, Blair was articulating a standard to which he and his colleagues could aspire. In the private sector, of course, the big picture question is usually 'will this create profits?'

The second can be a more operational goal. What are the key projects that need to be delivered? 'There is usually one thing which, if you can succeed in moving [it], moves everything else', says John Browne. 'For example, looking across government I said: "If there's one thing I want to achieve in year one it is to establish an academy to teach people how to lead major projects. Because if you get that right then most other things follow."' In Browne's view, every manager should have a clear view as to what this single thing is in their area.

When Heather Rabbatts became Chief Executive of Lambeth Council she recalls: 'Everything was out of kilter. The challenge was where to start.' She chose to tackle the high levels of staff sickness by disciplining those who showed unusual patterns of absenteeism. 'I knew that if I could shift that pattern of behaviour it would make a difference to performance. The people who were left carrying all the work but who would never stick their heads above the parapet to complain actually felt that somebody cared about them. So when all staff started thinking that they needed to turn up on time and work a full day, then people started to work even longer because they cared and things started to happen.'

The third big picture that came up was the personal big picture. What is the framework guiding your own decisions? 'The key question that any public servant needs to ask themself when making a decision,' says one manager 'is simply: can my minister/member defend this in public?' This mantra was repeated in one form or another by a number of people I interviewed. Many also ask themselves what the decision would look like if it appeared on the front page of a newspaper (*The Sun* and the *Daily Mail* were usually the newspapers of choice).

For Michael Bichard, the test is whether or not it is a decision with which he can personally live. This is not just for sentimental reasons but also for effective management and delivery: 'You're the person who has got to stand up in front of the council, the press, the profession, and defend the decision. And defending a decision that you actually don't agree with is horrible – people suss it.' He was describing this in the context of making a difficult decision when he was Chief Executive at the London Borough of Brent. The decision was whether or not to sack three social workers following a child abuse scandal. It was a no-win situation. On the one hand the press and members of the public were hounding him to act, and on the other hand the social care profession were warning him that to sack these people would be a betrayal of their profession. Having weighed up the arguments he ended up sacking the three workers because he instinctively knew that this was the decision he could live with and would feel comfortable defending and communicating.

Being clear, like Bichard, about these big-picture questions – whether strategic, operational or personal – helps you be clear about what decisions to take, particularly when the arguments on both sides may appear evenly balanced.

The decision-making framework of Paul Martin, Wandsworth Chief Executive

These are my operating principles, the sorts of things that are on my mind when I'm making a decision.

First, what is the customer perspective? I think it's important to break through provider self-interest and to have a view of the service user, the resident, the citizen and the impact of the decision on them.

The second would be to link it back to outcomes rather than judge it as a process.

A third would be about where the politicians come from on this; how interested they are in this issue, what level of involvement they need – do they need to be involved at all? Do they just need to be kept informed? Or do they need to be the co-architects of this decision?

A fourth would be about the culture of the organization that I'm working in and making sure that whatever decision is made is consistent with the way that people work in that organization. In most places, that will be about bringing people with you, understanding the reaction that the decision is likely to have and giving a lot of thought to how it's communicated and the staff ownership of it. So culture and staff ownership would be a fourth area.

And the fifth would be needing evidence about what others do on the issue. What is the experience of other councils, of other public sector bodies, of other organizations and having some kind of benchmarking or evidence base that enables me to test how it has gone down elsewhere.

Identify every potential point of view

Paul Roberts has started every new job by identifying his stakeholders. 'I invest heavily and personally in terms of time and empathy into understanding the different accountabilities and various groups and what they are looking for.' This serves him well when making decisions and indeed when working out what decisions to make in the first place. 'I would routinely, perhaps monthly, go through a checklist and make sure that I had within that period of time had at least some contact with each constituency of interest so that I hadn't lost sight or lost touch with some expectation. Also I never tried to take on a battle with more than one or two constituencies at a time because it seemed to me that if you took on more than two I always thought you were likely to meet a brick wall.'

'Dealing with a problem properly depends upon having all the arguments displayed and brought to the top for resolution', says Andrew Turnbull. He was reflecting on a decision made by the Department of the Environment when he was Permanent Secretary. The issue in question was how much to spend on roads and came at a time in 1997 when there was a high-profile wave of environmental protests featuring the likes of Swampy and Glenda Jackson. 'The roads budget had no friends but plenty of enemies. So its case wasn't argued and it was slashed despite the fact that 90 per cent of movement of goods and people is by road.' In retrospect, when making the decision, it would have been helpful to have engaged a champion for roads to make sure that all arguments were properly displayed.

In the 1980s when he was attempting to push through council housing legislation, Michael Heseltine sought champions of different points of view in a different way and for a different purpose. In this instance the decision – to allow council tenants to buy their home – had already been made, at least from his point of view. The challenge for Heseltine was to make sure that it could not be derailed. 'We knew that every Labour authority would try to frustrate this legislation and would crawl over it searching for loopholes. So I had the best legal advice from the department and all that. But I also asked my officials to go to the leading barrister in the housing field and retain him on the basis that his client is an extreme left-wing authority which is prepared to spend whatever it takes to break this legislation in the courts. And so his task is to show me how to break this legislation. And he did. And we blocked the loopholes and we won in the courts.'

So the lessons from these examples are to identify all potential stakeholders and ensure that their views are represented in the decision-making process, although sometimes it is not quite as simple as this. 'Many years ago I was the man stupid enough to think that the Huddersfield Hard of Hearing club and the Huddersfield Deaf Society might have a commonality of interest', says John Ransford. 'They were at absolute loggerheads and me trying to put them in one room for meetings was one of the worst mistakes of my professional life.' His conclusion is that while it is important to consult widely, it can be unhelpful to take the opinions of any one group or individual as final. 'People's views change. They are like you and me – we get influenced by different circumstances and different people.'

Focus your decision-making energies in the right areas

'The most urgent decisions are rarely the most important ones.' This dictum, ascribed originally to President Eisenhower, certainly has resonance for public sector managers who risk being dragged this way and that by events and media interest. Once you have a big-picture sense of direction and a framework against which to test your decisions, it is important to make sure you follow through without being distracted. One of Eisenhower's successors, President Obama, also recognizes the challenge of concentrating on the right decisions. 'I wear only gray or blue suits. I'm trying to pare down decisions. I don't want to make decisions about what I'm eating or wearing.... You need to focus your decision-making energy. You need to routinize yourself. You can't be going through your day distracted by trivia.'[3]

'Demand and context hugely affect which decisions get taken', says Richard Wilson. He points to the government's failure to make decisions about the future of nuclear power: it was never driven high enough up the agenda either by public demand or by any wider relevant government policy, for example about energy security. Wilson did his best to keep on top of decisions that needed to be taken but might slip below the radar by what he describes as 'surfing'. Two elements were critical. First of all, he would schedule regular meetings without any specific agenda throughout the government departments. These meetings allowed him to get a general sense of direction and what was going on without being drawn into the short-term issues. Secondly, at the end of every week he would produce a list of decisions – both long and short term – that needed to be taken by the prime minister and when they needed to be taken.

Others talk about the importance of having time for thinking and acting on important matters. Several managers specifically make space in their diaries to ensure that they do not get swept up in meetings and have time to deal with the most important rather than the most pressing issues. Chris Haskins is one who always makes sure he has some flexible time every day. He recalls approvingly that Tony Blair appeared to have this habit, whereas Gordon Brown did not. If he left a message asking to speak to Blair, he would invariably get a call back from Blair on the day and the issue would be dealt with. If he did the same with Brown, a meeting would be scheduled for several weeks hence.

> ### How Cabinet Secretary Richard Wilson managed his time and prioritized decisions
>
> *Every day I used to set out from home in a car from Buckinghamshire at 7.15. It took about an hour and a half and that was my thinking time because the morning is when your brain is clear. I would do my reading and then I would also have a list of all the current things which were on my mind. If you're in a situation of stress and managing a lot, the best secret is to write down everything that's worrying you. You write it down in order, and for me it used to come to between 30 and 50 items, and it would range from something big to something extremely small; something small could be the birthday of your driver and you've got to remember to get her a present, and then something big could be a White Paper.*
>
> *And then if you've written it all down you can work out which are the things you've got to do and you put a star by the ones you've got to do today; and probably there'll be eight stars typically which you've got to do, and probably another five that you would really be very happy if you did do. You probably aren't going to do more than 14 or 15, unless it's a really free day, a really good day. And in fact the first six things you do that day will not be on your list because other people need you to do something you've forgotten. But if you just have that concentration on eight things you will make sure they are done even if you end up delegating them. That's how I've always worked.*

Use scenarios

Many people I interviewed found it helpful when making decisions to think in terms of future scenarios. What would the repercussions and consequences of each decision be for different stakeholders? And what would happen if some of the assumptions that had been made turned out to be wrong?

'I like to do a little bit of testing and if there is one policy which comes out pretty well in a number of scenarios then I would feel pretty comfortable about that being the right one', says Gus O'Donnell. As an example he cited decisions made around welfare reform:

We were looking at incapacity benefit, how to get people onto it more quickly and how to tighten the rules so that there were proper medical checks. That was an interesting example where you started to say, okay but what if the medical checks don't work quite so well and some severely disabled people actually end up going to work so you're penalizing them when you shouldn't be. And what if we're going into a big recession and there is a big increase in unemployment so there are fewer jobs to go around anyway. Out of thinking about all these things, and more, we came to a policy which whilst still quite a tough policy was not as extreme as some of the ones that we thought up earlier.

Have lots of experience (or borrow it from somebody else)

One of the most annoying answers I received when I asked people how they made decisions was 'instinct'. This is annoying because it is not an easily transferable lesson. Of course, what they usually mean by instinct is experience or, as Peter Rogers puts it, 'they're not necessarily natural instincts, they're instincts acquired by watching really good people and how they deal with situations and how it feels'. Which is also not easily transferable and therefore almost as unhelpful for a young manager to hear.

'I wish my father was still alive because I owe him a big apology', says Ken Livingstone. 'I used to point to Alexander the Great and say that a 25-year-old could do anything, no problem. My dad would be much more cynical and would tell me there are just things that come with the passage of time and that you can't short circuit. And he was right. You can't teach in a university what a 25-year-old needs to know as a junior social worker about how to handle people. These things just come with experience. I was amazed at how much better I was at being mayor at 55 than I was at running the GLC at 35.'

So what can a young manager do to acquire such experience? Well, in one way not much. There is no way to gain experience other than, well, gaining experience. But it is possible to surround yourself with people who have this experience, either informally as mentors or more formally as advisers and even employees. In our consultancy we would frequently call upon senior retired public sector managers to help us on difficult projects. Invariably they were able to get on top of the issues and see solutions more quickly than we could. But what left more of a lasting impression on me was the skill they demonstrated when engaging and communicating with different audiences. They were invaluable. 'When you are young,' says Peter Rogers, 'you tend to believe that people over a certain age ought to be subject to euthanasia, but actually most of them have been there, done it and got the scars and I've learnt from a number of very good people in my time. But older managers can also learn from young people about energy, vision, using technology. There's a blend between new and old that adds value, and having the confidence and ability to talk to your bosses and bosses having the sort of humanity and sense to talk to the people they manage is part of the process.'

The good news is that it is easier than ever for younger managers to find support from more experienced people. In the public sector, retirement ages have not kept pace with the longer active lives that most of us are living thanks to better health care, diet and living conditions. If anything, the ages of our most senior managers and politicians are going down rather than up. The upshot is a growing body of retired public servants who remain at the top of their game and are often interested in passing on their expertise and instincts.

And what if you have to make a decision quickly?

You will not always be able to go through a long sensible consensus-building process for making decisions. Some decisions will not be important enough to justify the effort, others will simply happen too quickly.

Three things are important in these circumstances:

1 Check the financial and legal implications.

2 Always find time to talk to other people.

3 Where possible, engineer the chance to review the decision.

Of these, the most important is talking to other people.

Somebody who has experience of making important decisions under pressure is Charles Farr: 'For quick decision making my immediate reaction is to get lots of people together at once and involve more people than might otherwise be the case. Because someone's experience will be relevant.'

'When you don't have the time to do all the things the way you'd like to,' says Paul Martin, 'I think the key thing is who you speak to; who are the ones in any given situation whose view needs to be sought in order to make the right move. The riskiest position to be in is to take a decision without recourse to anyone else. Because you're trading then entirely on your own instincts and your own judgement.'

*

In February 2012, Helen Carter became Governor at Bullwood Hall Prison. 'I run an organization that makes decisions about risk every day, particularly about when and how to release prisoners', she says. 'When I read of a prisoner allowed out on Home Detention Curfew [prisoners who are allowed to live at home with an electronic tag] committing a serious offence, I hope that it's not one of mine.' Her decision making touches on many of the themes in this chapter.

First of all, she has processes which give her confidence. 'In reality you don't make the decision [about home detention curfews] alone. You will involve the offender manager who is a probation officer in the community. This person will visit the home, make an assessment and make recommendations to the prison. Equally, there is often input from a range of staff within the prison, and previous offences and conduct are taken into consideration. There is a clear process and there are forms to complete to ensure all aspects have been considered.'

Secondly, she has her own big-picture questions. 'I always think "If this splashes on the front of a newspaper, how will it be received?" I need to know that I'm spending public money in a way that can stand up in local or national media. And I also ask myself "Is this the right thing to do?", because morally I need to be able to go home and know that I've done the right thing.'

The third element is the importance of her own experience. In this case it is the importance of her experience in getting involved at appropriate moments and asking the questions when something tells her that the forms or process have not covered everything. She recounted a recent instance where a prisoner applied for an overnight stay with his mother. Normally, based on this prisoner's record, this would have been granted, 'but for some reason I didn't feel the process around home circumstances had been completed fully enough', says Carter. 'So I asked a bit more about the mum and it came back that she was a child minder who worked from home. This changed things. If the child goes home with a bruise that is unaccounted [for], who is the first person people will point the finger at? Also, I wouldn't be comfortable, as a parent of one of those children, knowing that somebody who is serving a current sentence is in the vicinity of my children. And so the answer was no.'

Summary

Decision making is difficult in the public sector, not just because of the complexity and significance of many decisions but also because there can be a natural bias against making decisions.

To help improve decision making:

- Just make decisions! Think about the impact that not making a decision might have, take comfort in the process you have gone through and remember that even if it goes wrong there may be extenuating circumstances.

- Focus your decision-making energy on the decisions which are most important to you and your organization.

- Invest time getting the data you need to make good decisions.

- Get inputs from different people, including: independent experts, champions for all sides of the debate, the people affected by the decision, and people with more experience than you.

- Be clear about your strategic, operational and personal priorities when making decisions.

- Where possible, consult people who have the experience of making similar decisions before.

- Are you spending your time and energy on the most important decisions?

- How clear are you about your overarching strategic, operational and personal goals? Do they help drive your decision making?

- Why can't you make the decision now?

- What is the impact of not making the decision?

- Even if you get the decision wrong, could you justify the process you have been through to reach it?

- Have you got as much data as you can feasibly get?

- Have you spoken to people whom the decision will affect?

- Have you spoken to champions of all points of view?

- Do you understand the legal and financial implications?

- Can you speak to people who have had experience of making this decision?

Notes

1 Rudolph Giuliani, *Leadership* (Miramax, New York, 2005), p 290.

2 Jonathan Powell, *The New Machiavelli: How to wield power in the modern world* (Vintage, London, 2011), p 46.

3 Obama's way – an interview by Michael Lewis, *Vanity Fair*, October 2012.

What the private sector can learn from the public sector

08

> *You don't want to get people in from the private sector, because people from the private sector very seldom understand the public sector. I think the transition is much easier the other way.*

NIGEL LAWSON

> *The private sector does not think highly of public sector management – they think they're not smart, flexible or decisive. The public sector thinks the private sector is corrupt. Neither is right.*

MICHAEL BLOOMBERG

> *I cannot think of a single skill that one needs in the private sector that people don't develop in spades in the public sector.*

IAN WATMORE[1]

So far this book has explored how public sector managers can improve their performance. This chapter is slightly different. Instead it looks at the ways in which public sector managers can help their private sector counterparts. In recent times the traffic in help and ideas has been pretty much one way, even though it has not always been successful or appropriate. 'I remember Thatcher getting terribly excited about the need to copy Marks & Spencer's', says Geoffrey Dear. 'A board-level director from Marks & Spencer's came and spent a long time with us and in the end went away, saying there is actually nothing that I can contribute because you are answerable and accountable in so many different directions.'

Michael Bichard attempted to even things up by trying to engage with Marks & Spencer's when he ran the Benefits Agency. Motivated at least partly by annoyance at being encouraged to emulate the retailer, he several times laid down a challenge: 'Give me 10 Marks & Spencer's staff and I'll put them in the Toxteth Benefit Office and I'll give you 10 of the Toxteth Benefit Office staff and let's see how they get on for a month.' The challenge was never taken up.

If they had taken up the challenge it is likely that the Marks & Spencer's staff would have learnt just as much from the Toxteth experience as vice versa. On a daily basis the Toxteth benefits officers would require high-quality decision making, smooth interpersonal skills and the ability to work under pressure. And yet the idea that the public sector might offer the private sector management advice does not have much traction, even among public sector managers.

At the end of every interview I asked the person I was interviewing what the private sector could learn from the public sector. Most looked puzzled. It was not something that they appeared to have thought much about before. Ask a private sector manager the question in reverse and you will immediately get responses including words like 'rigour', 'delivery' and 'focus'. And ask them what they think they might learn from the public sector and they will often come close to scoffing.

So what are these skills and experiences? And how might they be of practical use to the private sector?

The art of persuasion

In every organization there is a mix of persuasion and command and in government the former outweighs the latter.
NIGEL LAWSON

I quoted Michael Bloomberg earlier saying that one of the big differences between running a multi-billion-dollar business and being Mayor of New York is the sheer amount of communicating he has to do. This is partly because he is a politician. He has to tell the public personally what he is doing. But much of this relates to the persuasion that Nigel Lawson talks about. In many areas of his job Bloomberg cannot just order people to do what he wants. Instead, he spends large amounts of his time trying to gain the support and cooperation of different groups – other government agencies, businesses, communities – to achieve his goals.

Public sector managers will typically spend more time than their private sector counterparts seeking to persuade people – the public, politicians, colleagues, other government agencies, the media – to do things which help them achieve their goals. 'People in the private sector,' says Paul Martin, 'because they've got that lower level of accountability, are less likely to have thought hard about how they come across in public meetings, to camera, on a radio, in literature distributed to households.'

Brendan Barber has noticed the difference in persuasion skills between the managers he deals with in the private and the public sectors. 'People with key leadership responsibilities in the public sector are always conscious that they have to be persuaders and I don't think that's always the case in the private sector where people think they can sometimes funnel that stuff. They've got the job of making that decision, they make it, they tell everybody else just get on with executing it. This is such an important skill to have at times of change. Change just works so much better if people are actually bought into what you are trying to do, and if you can take them with you.'

Let me reiterate that, because it is on the face of it unconventional wisdom. In Barber's view the public sector's persuasive skills make them better equipped to deliver change than the private sector. But if you consider the ongoing changes which the public sector has to absorb and manage – demographics, technology, politics, the dreaded 'events' – and the scale on which they do it, then perhaps it is not such a startling observation to make. And yet you rarely hear of public sector managers being hired to deliver radical change in the private sector.

As an aside, Barber also sees a direct impact on the ability of private sector managers to negotiate in the area he knows best – industrial disputes. 'One of the things that slightly worries me about the private sector is the shortage of people with the experience of resolving serious disagreements. Sometimes in the private sector when I've been called in to help resolve disputes, I've been struck by how out of their depth some private sector management teams get. I think it's at least partly because they have no feel for the skills that you need to bring to bear to the industrial relations world.'

The persuasive skills of public sector managers will have been developed in dealing with partners. Public sector managers spend a considerable amount of time trying to create and sustain partnerships with other organizations – far more than most private sector managers. This is because so many public sector issues require a coordinated approach. You cannot tackle an issue like truancy, for example, without engaging with schools, social workers and even the police. Unlike the private sector, the public sector manager does not have the option of mergers or acquisitions – though there is always the option of restructuring. And the public sector manager does not usually get the chance to choose partners. If you are the borough commander in Tower Hamlets and don't get on with the chief executive or leader of the local authority, you can't very well go and partner instead with the chief executive of Cumbria County Council.

These factors all mean that public sector managers will on average spend more time getting partnerships to function effectively, no matter how tricky they may be. As a result, they are likely to be quicker and better at identifying the strengths, weaknesses and objectives of partners. They will be more adept at getting on with different stakeholders, wiser at knowing when and how to compromise and better at persuading partners to behave in ways that they want.

In a private sector context these persuasive skills are obviously useful for businesses that work closely with partners or with large multinational businesses that need to ensure that different parts of their organization work well together. They can also be useful for businesses undergoing restructuring, or merging with or acquiring other businesses. Or perhaps for businesses trying to break into new markets and build understanding of, and relationships in, those markets.

Generally, public sector managers will be adept at thinking about the more complex aspects of communicating and marketing. It is no longer enough for Tesco to be respected for providing the best products at the best prices; it needs to be admired and even loved. This can be a bottom-line issue – without this admiration Tesco may find it harder to get planning permission to develop as it would wish or it may find it harder to compete with local independent retailers.

Public sector managers have been grappling with these issues for years, even those not directly working in marketing and communications. They automatically think of all the different groups affected, how they might be affected, how they might respond in the short, medium and long term. They also are more experienced at trying to change public behaviour in complex ways. Whereas Tesco is trying to persuade us to buy our food there rather than at a competitor, the government might be trying to persuade us to drive more carefully, or eat more healthily. For a marketing and communications team to have this expertise would be even more useful now than it has ever been.

Making complex decisions

The head of Tesco's job is to get product on the shelf to deliver shareholder value. My job is to figure out how to generate growth among deprived communities who speak over a hundred different languages. NICK WALKLEY

I think if you've managed public risk and if you've managed across a complex range of issues that you bring a degree of lateralism and understanding of complex environments which I think have a place in the private sector.
HEATHER RABBATTS

Most public sector managers spend more time wrestling with tricky and significant decisions than their private sector counterparts. 'Public sector decision making is infinitely more complex than private sector', says Lord Heseltine. As Jonathan Powell puts it, 'Public sector managers need to be able to walk and chew gum at the same time.'

Ian Watmore is better placed than most to offer an opinion. He is an example of a manager who has worked successfully at senior levels in both the public and the private sectors. Before becoming a civil servant he was Managing Director for Accenture in the UK. Since that time he has had a number of public sector roles, including Permanent Secretary at what was then the Department for Innovation, Universities and Skills and then Chief Operating Officer for the Efficiency and Reform Group at the Cabinet Office. In among these jobs he also spent a year as Chief Executive of the Football Association. He says:

> I'm strongly of the view that the private sector is no better than the public sector. In some areas there are things that the public sector can manage more effectively than the private sector, in some areas it's the reverse and in many areas it's just different. I get really cross with my former private sector colleagues who just talk about government being incompetent or asleep at the switch, because it's just not true. Public

sector managers inherently manage within a complex environment and when the private sector gets into a complex environment it could take a lot of lessons from public sector colleagues. The public sector is very good at thinking long term, anticipating future problems and developing policies that work in all scenarios. It is inspirational to see, and very few people in the private sector do that with such skill.

So what does this mean in practice? What do public sector managers do when faced with a complex decision that private sector managers do not? And how might these skills be useful? When approaching a decision, public sector managers will typically consider the different stakeholders whom the decision might affect and the medium- to long-term external factors that might have an impact. They are likely to be adept at assessing how these different stakeholders – particularly those who are not customers – will respond. So, for example, in the context of a mobile telecommunications company, a public sector approach would be highly effective at anticipating how the behaviour of future customers might change in response to new technology and the impact this might have on communities, on the environment and on the way that people consume services. These insights could provide a valuable competitive edge.

And public sector managers are also likely to be good at consulting with different groups about decisions internally as well as externally. Instinctively they will seek out experts and people with an interest to test their ideas on. And they will be used to listening to this input and adapting their strategy accordingly. By contrast, it can be the case that in private sector organizations – even very large ones – there is a culture whereby important decisions can get made on the say-so of a tiny number of individuals. This is obviously useful for straightforward decisions but it can reduce the chances of getting the complex decisions right.

Crisis management

Most public sector managers will spend more time managing crises than their private sector counterparts. This is partly because public sector managers can be involved in so many life-altering situations and partly because they are more constantly under the glare of the media, particularly when things go wrong. Take a look at any newspaper or television news programme, local or national, and you will see that public sector organizations dominate the stories. As well as this general scrutiny, sometimes a major crisis will arise – a terrorist attack, abuse of a child in care, a virus outbreak – which will require rapid and assured decision making as well as careful handling of the media.

Thus a standard week for most leaders of public sector agencies will involve responding to publicity about something their organization has done. Sometimes this will require them to prepare politicians to respond and at other times they will be required to respond themselves. As well as responding to crises when they occur, crisis management will inform much of the planning and thinking. Public sector managers need to anticipate what would happen if things were to go wrong from an operational point of view and from a media perspective.

This experience means that when crises do arise, public sector managers are likely to be good at prioritizing what needs to be done, sure-footed in making sensible decisions quickly and effective at communicating with all the relevant stakeholders internally and externally.

*

There is obviously a risk of sweeping generalizations in comparing the relative merits of private and public sectors. There will be many private sector jobs which involve high levels of crisis management or partnership working. And it would be silly to suggest that a private sector manager would not have any of the skills of persuasion or complex decision making that are readily found in the public sector. It is, incidentally, equally silly to suggest that public sector managers are incapable of understanding balance sheets or imposing rigorous performance metrics.

But this chapter is really making two points. First of all, by virtue of the fact that many public sector managers do spend more of their time on certain management tasks than many of their private sector counterparts, unsurprisingly they are more skilled at doing them. Secondly, it would be helpful occasionally for private sector managers to think about how they could make use of these skills and ensure that traffic flows in both directions.

Note

1 This is an extract from a letter to the *Financial Times* on 25 February 2011.

Public sector managers and their public

09

In this final chapter I take a broader look at the world of public sector managers. I argue that:

- there is a significant discrepancy between the huge importance and difficulty of public sector management jobs and the relatively low status and respect they enjoy;

- this discrepancy is in part caused by making false and unflattering comparisons with the much more straightforward world of the private sector;

- and that we should take steps to address this by supporting public sector managers more, and perhaps increasing the salaries for senior public sector managers.

The importance of good public sector management

Imagine you could identify the thousand most talented managers in the country. How many would you want working in the public sector?

Most people would agree that good public sector management is important. But so, too, is good voluntary sector management. And clearly good private sector management is also vital, not least because it generates the money required to fund the public sector. We need good managers everywhere.

So what priority should we give to attracting and retaining good public sector managers? At senior levels the answer is top priority. It is hard to think of a private sector job that is more important or requires greater skill than running counter terrorism. Similarly, being Chief Executive of the Financial Services Authority or the National Health Service is a more significant and complex job than running any individual bank or pharmaceutical company. Even beyond the most senior levels, having good public sector managers around is vital for a number of reasons.

The public sector is often a monopoly provider

Many public sector services – rightly or wrongly – are monopolies. There is one financial regulatory system, one legal system, one army. Near where you live, there will typically be one police station, only one supplier of social workers and only one hospital. If any of these are managed poorly, we all suffer because we have nowhere else to turn.

By contrast, one of the major strengths of the private sector is its mutability and resilience. If Tesco performs poorly, Sainsbury's or Morrison's will pick up the slack.

Having a bad public sector manager presents a greater risk than having a bad private sector manager.

The financial impact is enormous

When things go wrong in the public sector, calculations are often made about how much it costs us all. The London Chamber of Commerce estimates that business in London loses £48m in productivity every day the Underground is not running. It is estimated that traffic congestion costs the British economy £20–30bn every year and that mental illness costs more than £70bn.

For regulation the numbers and guesses are exponentially wilder. Some suggest that the Sarbanes–Oxley Act of 2002, which increased the accounting demands placed on businesses, may have cost the US economy one trillion dollars (without helping it avoid the credit crunch). When it comes to the environment, Lord Stern estimates that without taking immediate action, climate change could reduce global GDP by 20 per cent ($10–15 trillion).

To put this in context, HSBC, currently the largest public British company by market capitalization, makes annual profits of just over £10bn. If the public sector could halve the costs of mental health – just one of many areas of illness – it would be contributing the same amount to the economy as three HSBCs.

The comparison is not a perfect one. In the case of HSBC wealth is being created, whereas in the case of mental health costs are being avoided. However, in areas of regulation the distinction is less clear. You could argue, for example, that the way a government manages planning regulation might create wealth or at least might set the conditions for creating wealth.

But the main point is that the public sector very often has a financial impact on a scale far greater than any individual private sector business, which is why, again, good management is vital.

It determines our quality of life

At a more fundamental level, quite simply the public sector shapes many of the most important things in our daily lives: what our environment looks like, how we move around, our health, our education, even our cultural lives. It also looks after the more vulnerable people in our society – the chronically sick, the elderly – and protects us from the most dangerous. Few individuals have the opportunity to affect the quality of these day-to-day experiences more than our local public servants, whether in the local authority, in the local police force or in the local health service.

Nationally, the public sector sets and enforces the legal framework which ensures that we can own homes, set up businesses, employ people and be employed. And, of course, it has the responsibility of keeping our homes and our workplaces safe from terrorist attacks.

In all these areas – local and national – the quality of the management will affect the quality of our lives.

Globalization makes good public sector management even more important

"I would like to come back as the bond market. You can intimidate everybody. JAMES CARVILLE, FORMER ADVISER TO PRESIDENT CLINTON

We are incredibly interdependent and have become more so – just look at the impact the fuel tanker blockade had on everything... the private sector cannot thrive unless everything else works and the public sector has to make it work. ANDREW TURNBULL

Power lists are increasingly dominated by business people. However spuriously these lists are compiled, they do reflect a trend. Businesses – particularly those involved in media or financial services – have become more influential as it becomes easier to move information and money, not to mention people and corporate headquarters, around the world.

Thus when the British government develops new frameworks for tax, or for law or for financial services, the stakes are higher and the process is more complicated. The government has to take into account the frameworks available in other countries and develop policies which will make the United Kingdom an appealing place for all sorts of businesses. For the same reason it is crucial that our physical infrastructure remains attractive. We will increasingly be compared to other countries on the quality of our transport, our education, our health-care system, our environment and even our cultural attractions.

Many of the most important issues that face Britain also have a global complexion. The ability of our public sector managers, together with our politicians, to negotiate successfully on issues like climate change, banking regulation and counter-terrorism will determine our prosperity, safety and quality of life. These are not straightforward topics in their own right and they are not made easier by negotiating with other nations who have different systems, different values and for that matter different languages. Has there ever been a private sector meeting as complicated or as important as the negotiations at the climate conference in Copenhagen?

As the direct power of governments has weakened, the need for skills to influence has grown. And as the demand for multinational solutions to multifaceted problems has increased, so too has the need for managers who can handle increasingly complex analysis and negotiation. Good public sector management is more important than ever.

The status of public sector managers

Despite the complexity of the jobs they do, and despite the obvious importance of these jobs, public sector managers do not often enjoy a very good reputation.

I did not expect to think much about this book when I visited Suzhou Industrial Park in 2011. Suzhou is yet another enormous Chinese city which remains largely unknown to westerners. It is 75 miles from Shanghai, has a population of 10 million and is growing fast. Within China it is famed for its beauty: '*Up in the sky there is heaven, down on earth there is Suzhou.*' I am a director of a business started up by a Chinese friend and I was there to meet the government official in charge of the Industrial Park. The meeting started at 4 o'clock in the afternoon and we emerged two and a half hours later. My friend's first reaction, much to the amusement of his colleagues, was to express surprise that the meeting had lasted so long: 'I can't believe that someone in the government was prepared to work past 5 o'clock.' It was both reassuringly familiar and a little depressing to find that mild mockery of public sector managers is as alive and well in China as it is in the United Kingdom.

In the UK, it can sometimes appear that even the public sector lacks confidence in itself. A survey by the Institute of Leadership and Management[1] revealed that relative to workers in the voluntary and private sectors, public sector workers trust their managers less and have less faith in their abilities. 'The civil service has encouraged a view which says you go to the private sector for best practice', says David Normington. There is further evidence to support his opinion. The public sector is constantly seeking the help of the private sector. The government appoints people from the private sector directly as ministers or as senior civil servants. Successful private sector figures are asked to write important reports which often translate into legislation. And recently, with the help of Lord Browne of Madingley – the former Chief Executive of BP – the government has appointed non-executive directors to the boards of government departments. Of 59 appointed so far, 51 have had their primary professional experience in the private sector.

It is, of course, sensible to seek advice from outsiders. But what is bizarre is how one way the traffic is. 'Business has been brought up to think that Whitehall is useless', says Chris Haskins, and again the evidence would bear him out. Among the FTSE 100 companies there are no chief executives who have come directly from the public sector. In 2011, among almost 800 non-executive directors in the FTSE 100, I could find only five former permanent secretaries and no former local government chief executives. A survey run jointly by Barclays and the *Financial Times* in 2011 suggested that more than half of businesses were not very interested (25 per cent) or not at all interested (32 per cent) in taking on people who had lost their jobs in the public sector as a result of cuts.[2] In short, the private sector appears to have little interest in using the expertise and experience of public sector managers.

A Boston Consulting Group (BCG) report from February 2012, which compares civil service attitudes to their jobs with their private sector counterparts, adds further fuel. Perhaps the most remarkable finding is that 54 per cent of civil servants are proud to work for their organization, compared to 82 per cent in the private sector. This may seem counterintuitive. Surely if there is one area in which you could guarantee that the public sector would score more highly than the private sector it would be pride? Working for the public good must be more fulfilling than making money for shareholders? Well, according to this survey, apparently not. And it is not uncommon to meet public sector workers who arm themselves against any criticism with self-deprecating comments about their workplace.

On a financial level there is no contest among senior managers. In 2011, the average FTSE 100 chief executive earned £4.8m. In the same year the top public sector salary by several hundred thousand pounds was the £622,000 earned by the Director General of the BBC. The Cabinet Secretary, the country's most senior civil servant who sits on top of a budget of £600bn and 6 million employees, received £285,000 – 6 per cent of the average FTSE 100 chief executive salary.

Even at the lower end of the FTSE 100 pay-scale the discrepancy is significant. Compare Andy Harrison and Stephen Hughes. Harrison is Chief Executive of Whitbread, which describes itself as the power behind some of the United Kingdom's most successful hospitality brands, including Premier Inn and Costa Coffee, and employs more than 40,000 people. In the year ending April 2012, Whitbread had revenues of just under £1.8bn and profits of £320m. Hughes is the Chief Executive of Birmingham City Council. The council delivers more than 600 different services, including looking after vulnerable children and the elderly, managing the city's transport infrastructure and delivering education. His budget in 2011 was £3.5bn and he employs more than 50,000 people. In the year ending April 2012, Harrison earned £1,159,000 and two other executives earned £1,981,000 and £2,465,000. Hughes' earnings in 2011 were £233,000.

Two things are striking about this. The first is the disparity in financial rewards: Harrison earns almost five times more than Hughes and one of his colleagues earns more than ten times as much. The second is that in every respect the job that Hughes does is bigger, more important and more complicated.

Backgammon versus chess – unfair comparisons with the private sector

Although there are logical, market-driven reasons for private sector managers to earn more than their public sector counterparts, it is less clear why public sector managers should not get more respect. One answer is ideological. 'There's no doubt that Thatcher set out deliberately to try to make public service less attractive and to try to make private sector more attractive', says Jonathan Powell. 'It was a deliberate ideological aim and she achieved it and that wasn't necessarily a bad thing at the time.' Those who, like Thatcher, are committed to the idea of small government have an interest in continuing to highlight the inefficiencies of the public sector relative to the private sector. And the public sector almost always suffers badly by comparison. 'I feel very strongly,' says Nick Walkley, 'that we have begot an era where people create legitimacy by doing down public service.'

This doing down of the public sector by comparison with the private sector has become commonplace. In March 2012, the National Audit Office (NAO) published a report assessing the progress made by five Whitehall departments in implementing shared service centres. These centres bring together the disparate back office functions, such as human resources, finance and procurement, into one organization in order to save money and improve services. The report was challenging and largely critical of the progress made. It was, as most NAO reports are, credible, detailed and constructive.

Except for one element. At the start the report states that 'the private sector has typically saved in excess of 20 per cent [from implementing shared services], with a less than five year return on investment'. Later on it returns to the theme: 'Our analysis... shows implementation projects have been expensive, with lengthy anticipated and actual break-even periods ranging from four to eight years. Typically, shared service centres in the private sector target and achieve less than five years to break even.' The accompanying press release also draws attention to the comparison. 'While, in one instance government has achieved break-even in a time consistent with the private sector, its overall performance has been varied.'

What relevance did this comparison have? It is very hard to tell, because the report provides no context. The betting probability is that the projects in the private sector were nothing like as large and complex as those covered by the NAO report. The betting certainty is that none of them were being implemented under similar levels of governance and accountability. I do not for one moment think that the NAO was deliberately trying to draw unfair comparisons. In fact, for such a distinguished, impressive and independent body as the NAO to make these comments just shows how such false comparisons have become second nature.

This is unfortunate. It is like comparing backgammon and chess and concluding that Gary Kasparov is unimpressive because his games take too long and sometimes end in draws. We can see this mentality seeping in whenever public sector bodies are excoriated for being overly bureaucratic or for not having clear impact measures or a good return on investment. Sometimes, of course, such criticisms are valid but often they will not take account of the additional bureaucracy necessary for a publicly accountable body, nor of the challenge of applying numerical rigour to things that cannot sensibly be measured. The risk is that without context we are left with the impression, as in the NAO report, that the public sector is less competent that the private sector when in fact what they are attempting is simply harder to achieve.

In October 2010, Sir Philip Green followed in the footsteps of many other successful business figures by agreeing to write a report for the government. His task was to conduct an efficiency review of government spending. Speaking about his findings Sir Philip said: 'The process is shocking. There's no reporting, there's no accountability.... You could not be in business if you operated like this. It would be impossible.'

Certainly the analysis set out in the report of the problems with public sector procurement is robust and damning. Sir Philip finds embarrassing examples of inefficiencies – some government departments paying £8 for a box of paper, others paying £73 – and problems with poor data and poor coordination of procurement. His solutions to these problems appear seductively sensible: Sir Philip recommends centralizing and coordinating purchasing, improving data quality and making use of the government's credit rating and scale to drive down prices. 'There is no reason,' he writes, 'why the thinking in the public sector needs to be different from the private sector.'

In my opinion it is not safe to assume that democratically elected bodies have the simple objective of achieving the best prices. Although price will be a key factor, they will also be using their procurement to support wider, more complex objectives. Some will be strategic – investing in training and infrastructure; others may be more short term and politically driven, for example supporting local businesses rather than shopping abroad. Crucially, they will vary from area to area.

Furthermore, I doubt that it is simple or cheap to centralize in the way that Sir Philip envisages. There are different systems for collecting data, different approaches to calculating overheads, different types of contracts in place with different suppliers, different processes for procurement and even different definitions for purchase items. It is not straightforward to get rid of these differences, owing to the sheer size and diversity of the public sector as well as its multifaceted governance. The public sector spends £670bn every year, employs more than 6 million people, provides thousands of services and has a highly complex system of accountability. No business comes close to this in scale or complexity. Sitting in the middle, the Prime Minister or the Cabinet Secretary cannot command the public sector in the way that chief executives can command their companies. And so the challenges specific to the public sector – no single success criterion, democratic accountability, scale and complexity – make even apparently straightforward areas such as procurement exponentially more difficult.

The adversarial nature of our politics and the media coverage of the public sector exacerbate this. Every day we read, watch or hear our government being criticized by the opposition, no matter what they are doing. Our media tend to cover what is going wrong because it is more interesting. Who wants to read about another good day for the transport infrastructure? Certainly we are very poorly informed about some of the major aspects of public sector work. People consistently have a far more negative view of issues such as crime, immigration and family breakdown than is warranted by the reality. More trivially, one survey[3] suggests that 25 per cent of the public think people who run public sector organizations are paid more than their private sector counterparts and just 36 per cent think they are paid less. This public ignorance is deeply depressing in itself. Why is a country with so many press freedoms so poorly informed? From a public sector point of view, this bias towards the negative must also contribute to the perception we have about the competence of public sector managers.

High importance, (relatively) low status – does it matter?

On the one hand, we have important jobs in the public sector which require enormous skill and commitment. On the other hand, the roles themselves appear to attract little respect and relatively little financial reward. This is an unpromising combination. How can we be sure that the public sector is attracting and retaining the most talented people?

It is hard to assess the quality of people working in or entering the public sector. At entry level, the number of applicants to the civil service with first-class degrees from Russell Group universities has never been higher.[4] Anecdotally, many of the people I interviewed who had experience in both the private and public sectors extolled the qualities of public sector workers. Michael Barber is a good example of this when he says that 'civil servants are about as talented a group of professionals as I know. If I had to rank professions in this country on talent, civil servants would be near the top.' Like Barber, I have also met huge numbers of the most impressive people I know working in the public sector. And yet equally anecdotally, many who do not work in the public sector – and indeed a large contingent who do – are less impressed. In the BCG report quoted earlier, public sector managers scored poorly relative to their private sector counterparts on leadership, communications and commitment to organizational goals and values.

But my concern is the next generation. Are the exceptional people currently in their mid-20s attracted to the public sector? The UK graduate careers survey in 2009 suggested that just 22 per cent of graduates think it is prestigious for high-fliers to join the public sector, although 69 per cent think it retains 'real status and kudos'. A survey of Young Global Leaders[5] – a group set up by the World Economic Forum for 'exceptional young leaders who share a commitment to shaping the global future' – is more damning. While 76 per cent of the 300 who took part in the survey would consider working in public office, just 5 per cent were currently doing so. This is admittedly a global group so it is hard to untangle specific lessons for the United Kingdom, but what is significant is that these are not just high-fliers but high-fliers who want to make a difference – and yet even for these people the public sector is not attractive.

Jonathan Powell recalls a conversation from his time at Morgan Stanley:

> I was in a taxi with a young person who had a very strong Scottish accent and clearly had a working-class background. He said to me: 'Why do people go into the civil service? When I was at university it never even occurred to me to think of going into the civil service.' I said 'Public service' and he said 'What?' and I said 'Public service – they have this ethos' and he had no comprehension of what I was talking about; he just could not understand why anyone would want to go into anything as boring as the civil service.

At the opposite end of the scale Charles Guthrie reports a similar experience. 'I went down to Eton the other day and asked the headmaster: "What do your bright boys want to do?" I was delighted that the same sort of numbers wanted to go into the army. Some wanted to go into investment banking... Some of his very brightest and best wanted to go into the media... He had three boys in five years who wanted to go into the Foreign Office. He had not a single boy who wanted to go into the Home Civil Service.' Neither the anecdotes nor the numbers are conclusive, nor are they ever likely to be. Assessing the managerial qualities of human beings is an imprecise science. So, does it matter? My answer is an unequivocal yes. Even though the evidence is inconclusive, we can say two things for certain: first, that the benefits of good public sector managers are enormous; second, that we are manifestly not doing our best to make the roles attractive. In risk-register terms, the potential impact of less good public sector managers in the future is very high. The challenge is that, as we have seen, the likelihood is hard to assess and arguably low. The worry is that it is not easy to reverse. If the calibre of public sector managers declines in the next 30 years the impact will creep up on us. And, like the frog splashing lazily around in the slowly heating water, we may not notice it until it is too late to do anything about it.

Making the public sector more attractive – better status, better pay

So what can be done to make the public sector more attractive? It is beyond the remit of this book and beyond the expertise of its author to come up with any hard and fast answers, but here are some 'dipping toe in the water' thoughts.

Let us go back to the survey of Young Global Leaders. Given that so many of them would consider working in public office, why don't they? The survey gives the following answer: 'They are deterred from entering the public sector due to the high level of bureaucracy, lack of a true meritocracy, low financial compensation, widespread fraud and corruption and constant public scrutiny.'

Leaving fraud and corruption to one side, what leaps out from this fairly comprehensive list is how little the public sector can do to deal with these objections. There will always be greater levels of bureaucracy and public scrutiny. It will always be harder to discern talent in a system where it is difficult to untangle individual contributions to complex outcomes and where people are vulnerable to changing and changeable politicians. Which leaves financial compensation. Should we pay our senior public sector managers more? There are a number of objections to doing so.

First of all, as already discussed, it is not obvious that there is a problem. Applications for jobs in the public sector remain high and it is hard to prove that the calibre of top public sector managers is any less good than that of top private sector managers.

Secondly, paying more money is not a failsafe way to attract better people. Money is, after all, only one factor in the decisions people take about where they work, albeit an important one. Some might even argue (unconvincingly in my view) that high salaries could put off excellent people by undermining the culture and ethos of public sector service.

The third – and most significant – obstacle is the public appetite for such a move. By almost any standards the salaries at the top of the public sector are excellent. There is not a lot of sympathy for people earning six-figure salaries. One senior civil servant said to me:

'We have a salary scale that means Permanent Secretaries cannot afford to live with their families in central London.' This is not a complaint that would be happily received by the public. And, of course, politicians compete with each other to curb what they call the excesses of the public sector fat cats.

The final challenge is coming up with a reasonable way of valuing what they should be paid. Efforts to tie this to their financial impact are pretty hopeless – how do you assess the impact that any one individual has in such a complex system? Equally, those critics who say that public sector managers are being paid the market rate – 'If they think they can earn more then get the private sector to pay them more' – miss the point. Once you become a senior public sector manager then no matter how good you are, for all but a tiny minority, the only jobs you are really qualified to do are those in the public sector. Setting the salaries is about attracting the next generation into the public sector, not (with apologies to the current senior public sector managers) supporting this generation.

Perhaps there might be some way of benchmarking public sector pay against the private sector by comparing the size, the importance and the complexity of individual organizations. Public sector managers could then have their salaries tied in some way to a basket of different organizations – for example by receiving no more than 25 per cent of the average salary and no less than 20 per cent.

More importantly, it will take some very brave and talented politicians to make the case to the public that it is in all our interests for this to change, because the argument is based on a hunch. And the hunch is that by paying much better wages, we will attract and retain better people. And that by having better people we will reduce the chances of terrorist attacks, we will increase the quality of education, we will provide better support to vulnerable people, we will make it more likely that we can come up with a sensible approach to climate change and can create the right conditions for prosperity.

There is support for higher salaries from an unlikely quarter. Ken Livingstone caused consternation when he appointed Bob Kiley to run Transport for London in 2001 and paid him a salary just under £500,000. 'I am quite prepared to pay people of outstanding talent whatever it takes to bring them to work', says Livingstone. 'One of the ways in which the civil service has lost its dynamism is to set these very restricted pay levels so the best will not apply.'

According to Jonathan Powell, Blair agreed with this approach:

> One of the things that Tony used to always say is that we should pay someone a huge amount of money to go away and solve the problem. In terms of saving the public purse, it wouldn't matter at all if you paid someone two or three million pounds a year to do that if they did it properly. But we have this strange mentality in Britain when we always celebrate when the neighbour's pig dies. So if anyone gets paid a lot it causes a huge political issue and we all make a fuss. But in fact, from the point of view of the ordinary taxpayer, you ought to be delighted if you've got someone that's going to be paid a lot of money if they actually achieve something.

Even somebody as committed to public service as Livingstone himself recognizes the personal attractions of money: 'What I have always wanted was power but you also need a bit of money. There are those people who make a lot of money and then come into public service. In retrospect, if I had my life again, I might do that.' His more extreme opponents might be cheered by the thought that future Livingstones could be deterred from entering public life for financial reasons. But, for most, I think this is could be one more indicator that it might be worth looking again at the way that we reward our senior public sector figures.

Logistically, if not politically, it is very easy to increase pay. It is far less easy to improve the levels of respect that public sector managers enjoy, although it may arguably be more important. For starters, respect is a fairly nebulous concept measured by surveys or by proxy indicators such as the number of non-executives employed by FTSE 100 companies. In addition, the levers for improving respect are imprecise and uncertain. The media in all its guises is probably one such lever, money itself might be another, and so too perhaps are politicians. My final hope for this book is that in its own very small way it might also be one of these levers which contributes towards a growing respect for what public sector managers do.

Notes

1 Institute of Leadership and Management, *Index of Leadership Trust 2011* (ILM, London); 2,500 managers were surveyed of whom 40 per cent were from the public sector.

2 Barclays Corporate and Financial Times Job Creation Survey 2011.

3 A YouGov/ITV poll in October 2009.

4 Will Hutton, Final Report of his Independent Review into Fair Pay in the Public Sector (HM Treasury, London, March 2011), p 62.

5 PwC and the World Economic Forum Young Global Leaders network, *The War for Talent Goes Public* (PwC, London, 2011).

Conclusion

At the start of the book I made the point that perhaps the single biggest lesson to take from it is that there is no single approach to managing in the public sector. This reflects the inherent individuality of management – different approaches will suit different people – as well as the huge size and variety of activity within the public sector.

Nonetheless, there were four key bits of advice to which I return here. These bits of advice help public sector managers deal with the management challenges which arise from working in an environment which lacks a single simple measure of success and is democratically accountable. In each case they refer to activities that public sector managers should be thinking about or doing more than their private sector counterparts:

1 **Exploit the limitless comparative data.** Almost every aspect of management can be made easier by having timely and accurate information about your peers. Whether it is setting targets, assessing performance or identifying innovations, access to these comparative data is an extraordinary windfall for public sector managers. This is not just about learning from others. It is also about introducing competition and accountability. If the public and politicians can compare performance, they will demand more of organizations and individuals that fall behind, and praise organizations that perform well.

   As we have seen, the police use comparisons of crime data to hold the performance of individual areas to account and to identify pockets of best practice which can be shared. Local authority managers like Nick Walkley can use the data to drive performance in areas as diverse as waste management and council tax collection. And as Michael Barber showed, these comparisons need not be limited to the United Kingdom but could extend to mobile phone theft in New York or railway systems in Poland.

It is the single most effective way of meeting the challenges of democratic accountability and not having a bottom line. However, too often this fantastic resource is not fully exploited. Too often the information is patchy or poorly presented. Too often managers do not invest the necessary time and money in chasing good information and interpreting it. Too often they can be held back from publishing information about their relative performance by the fear that it will be (wilfully) misunderstood. These excuses, though valid, do not stand up against the huge benefits that this information can bring. Managers should prioritize getting the data that they need, in the words of Michael Barber 'through sheer bloody-mindedness'.

2 **Link people vividly to the ultimate impact of what they do.**
One of the pleasures of working in the public sector is that the primary outcome of your work is to help your fellow citizens in some way rather than to make money. This should be a source of huge motivation and inspiration and yet, as we have seen, studies show that often private sector workers are more motivated and inspired by what they do.

For doctors, nurses and teachers the impact and motivation are very tangible – the recuperating patient, the developing child. But in many areas of the public sector the link is less obvious. Prison officers spend the bulk of their time with offenders and, depressingly, with re-offenders rather than with reformed prisoners and the families of victims. Before he arrived there, Michael Bichard's civil servants at the Department of Education did not routinely see the insides of the classrooms which were being shaped by the policies they were creating.

Public sector managers should think hard about how they can regularly bring their staff (and themselves) closer to the people who are benefiting from their work. This can happen through spending time with people on the frontline, as Geoffrey Dear did regularly with his police officers or as Kevan Collins did during the *Undercover Boss* television programme. It can be encouraged, as Bichard did at the Department for Education and as Charles Farr does formally through his emphasis on relationship building with stakeholders in his set of corporate values. But it can also happen in other less direct ways. A doctor told me of the pleasure that she and her colleagues would get from receiving and then sharing letters from grateful patients.

This contact achieves two things – it is useful because it provides a source of information about how they can serve their beneficiaries better and it is inspiring because it can remind people about the force for good that they can be.

3 **Getting soft feedback on the soft stuff.** The public sector can rarely be held to account just by using numerical measures. Instead of spending time developing more complex levels of numerical reporting, public sector managers could think about ways of getting consistent feedback on the softer aspects of performance. This happens in small ways already. Citizens are asked to give subjective judgements about how satisfied they are with their local authority, how cohesive they think their community is or how safe they feel. For individuals, 360-degree feedback – whereby people receive feedback from their bosses, their peers and their staff – is also used sporadically.

But there is scope to make such feedback wider and deeper and to embed it more firmly in management processes. Organizations and individuals could systematically seek feedback from partners, colleagues, suppliers, citizens and their direct peers. The areas covered may well be subjective – How well do I/does the organization manage relationships? How good is the analysis? How reliable are we/am I? How good is decision making and prioritizing? – but the systematic feedback will make it easier to have the sorts of honest conversations about performance which are hugely important but often avoided.

More generally, like Paul Roberts with his mental Geiger counter, managers should consciously be seeking feedback from their day-to-day interactions with staff, with customers and with colleagues. Such systematic and conscious feedback is one more way of managing in an environment which will not offer you the thumping feedback of the bottom line.

4 **Be proactive!** It is sometimes easy not to do things in the public sector. Not to make a decision, not to take a risk, not to deal with poor performance. The successful managers I know all seem to me to be doers. When Helen Bailey is deciding to let the Arsenal parade take place or ignoring statutory requirements to get a deal done, she is relying on her instincts and judgements and her desire to make things happen. When Michael Bichard focuses in interviews on what people have achieved rather than the positions they have held, he is trying to identify this quality in others. When Michael Bloomberg describes the way he rapidly and enthusiastically adopts innovations that his employees suggest, he too is demonstrating this quality and how it can be encouraged in others.

This is not a straightforwardly transferable skill. It is more a mindset. In the face of complex governance, onerous bureaucracy and understandable risk aversion, proactive managers will always be focused on how they can achieve useful things through their energy, imagination and intuition.

In the Introduction to this book I pointed out the dominance of management books about the private sector. This echoes the wider dominance enjoyed by senior private sector managers when it comes to pay and status. This dominance has another, more insidious effect. Many of the private sector notions of good management have hijacked language and thinking about management generally. Of course, this is useful in some cases. But in other instances it can be less useful.

And yet in many of the areas covered in this book, particularly the four areas highlighted in the conclusion, the public sector should be developing new ways of working. These should go far beyond anything that the private sector either has done or is capable of doing, either because it lacks the pressure to do so (thanks to the bottom line, the private sector does not have to think as hard about the soft stuff) or because it lacks the resources (eg the limitless comparative data).

In years to come therefore, bookshelves should be heaving with public sector management books which will be pored over by public and private sector managers alike.

I hope you have enjoyed the book and found it useful. Please feel free to get in touch with comments or suggestions via my website, **www.alexanderstevenson.co.uk,** or via Twitter, @alsteve1.

TWENTY-FIVE KEY INSIGHTS

In no particular order, here is a list of 25 key insights both large and small that have cropped up during the book:

1 Avoid setting targets if you can; drive performance by monitoring data instead.

2 If you are setting targets, try to make them radical and ambitious, not day to day and operational.

3 Think about what you need to measure, not what you can measure, and then work out how to get that data.

4 In any mission statement or strategy, emphasize the inspiring ways in which you are improving lives.

5 Where possible, use your politicians to test new ideas or to seek feedback on your behalf on existing projects from the public – they are a great bridge to your customers.

6 At the start of new initiatives, think hard about how you can develop counterfactuals to demonstrate the impact that you are having.

7 Find out about the personal background and experiences of your politicians so that you can understand them and get the most out of them.

8 Ask colleagues what they have learnt from their appraisals; this will be useful in itself and reinforce the importance of appraisals within the organization.

9 Give new members of staff a project to do for you so that you can get a sense of their strengths and weaknesses.

10 Encourage your staff to spend time informally with their stakeholders to build the trust and understanding they will need when the relationships come under pressure.

11 Think of your own working relationships in terms of trust – whom do you trust and who trusts you – so that you can work out where you need to spend time.

12 Recruit people who can demonstrate their ability to take decisions.

13 When recruiting, test what people have achieved; do not be seduced by the posts they have held nor their plans for the future.

14 If people – and especially colleagues – give you what turn out to be misleading references, make sure you challenge them about it robustly.

15 Use organograms as a starting point for understanding the size, shape and efficacy of an organization.

16 Proactively seek opposing views to the key decisions that you make.

17 If you have to make an important decision quickly, spend what little time you have talking to as many people as possible before making it.

18 Confront poor performance; colleagues will be grateful, standards generally will rise and you will save time in the long run.

19 When promoting somebody, make sure that the rest of your team understands why – use it as an opportunity to demonstrate what you value.

20 Send general update e-mails out on Friday – people are more likely to reflect and draw conclusions on their own over the weekend than by discussing them immediately with colleagues.

21 When considering how to handle a poor performer, think in terms of skills (which you can usually develop) and values (which you usually cannot).

22 When starting a new role, draw up a list of your stakeholders; review it regularly to check that you are engaging with them all appropriately.

23 Seek advice from people with more experience than you; retired public servants can be particularly valuable confidants.

24 Stimulate new ideas by inviting outsiders to talk to your organization about what they do.

25 Stimulate new ideas by bringing your frontline staff face to face with end users to discuss how to improve services.

INTERVIEWEE BIOGRAPHIES

Helen Bailey is Chief Executive of Local Partnerships. She was previously Director of Public Services at HM Treasury, responsible for spending on local government, housing, health and education. She was Chief Executive in the London Borough of Islington from 2002 to 2008. Prior to that, Helen had a career in public service and management consultancy.

Stephen Bampfylde is co-founder and Chairman of Saxton Bampfylde. He began his career working for IBM and Whitehall, where he spent nearly 10 years before moving into top-level executive search. For 25 years he has been involved in the recruitment of executives to senior positions across all sectors. He helped establish the worldwide professional association AESC in Europe and was its international director for a number of years. Outside executive search, he has been involved with the advisory boards of the business schools at Cambridge and City Universities, is a Trustee of the Yvonne Arnaud Theatre, and Chairman of the Guildford Cathedral Council.

Brendan Barber was General Secretary of the Trade Unions Congress between 2003 and 2012. He began working there in 1975.

Sir Michael Barber served the UK government as Head of the Prime Minister's Delivery Unit (from 2001 to 2005) and as Chief Adviser to the Secretary of State for Education on school standards (from 1997 to 2001). He is currently Chief Education Adviser at Pearson and was a Partner at McKinsey & Company and Head of McKinsey's global education practice. He is also Distinguished Visiting Fellow at the Harvard Graduate School of Education and is the author of several books, including *Instruction to Deliver*; *The Learning Game: Arguments for an education revolution*; and

How to do the Impossible: A guide for politicians with a passion for education.

Lord (Michael) Bichard spent 30 years working in the public sector. He was Chief Executive of Brent and Gloucestershire Local Authorities and in 1990 became Chief Executive of the government's Benefits Agency. In 1995 he was appointed Permanent Secretary of the Employment Department and then the Department for Education and Employment, before leaving the civil service in 2001. Since then he has been Rector of the University of the Arts, Director of the Institute for Government, Chair of the Legal Services Commission and Chairman of the Design Council.

Michael Bloomberg is the 108th Mayor of the City of New York. He was first elected in November 2001 and has been re-elected twice since then. Before entering politics he set up the global media company Bloomberg.

Lord (John) Browne of Madingley is the government's lead non-executive director and has been managing the appointment of non-executive directors to the board of each government department. He is presently a Partner of Riverstone Holdings LLC, a company which invests in renewable and conventional energy. He is Chairman of the Board of Trustees of Tate, immediate past President of the Royal Academy of Engineering, Chairman of the advisory board of the Blavatnik School of Government, Oxford, and a member of a variety of other boards. He was Group Chief Executive of BP between 1995 and 2007.

Lord (Robin) Butler had a high-profile career in the civil service from 1961 to 1998, serving as Private Secretary to five prime ministers and Cabinet Secretary to a further two. He was secretary of the Cabinet and Head of the Home Civil Service from 1988 to 1998.

Helen Carter joined the Prison Service in September 2002, after completing a BA (Honours) in Business Studies at Sheffield Hallam University, directly on to the Accelerated Promotion Scheme (APS).

After working in a number of prisons in the northwest she then moved to the east of England to lead an expansion project at HMP Littlehey. With the expansion complete she then took over the role of Deputy Governor at HMP/YOI Littlehey and moved to HMP Bullwood Hall where she became Governor in 2012.

Charles Clarke was Home Secretary between December 2004 and May 2006. Prior to that, he was Secretary of State for Education and Skills from October 2002. He was Member of Parliament for Norwich South for 13 years and a councillor in Hackney for 6 years.

Sir Merrick Cockell was elected Local Government Association Chairman in 2011. He has been Leader of the Royal Borough of Kensington and Chelsea since 2000 and first became a councillor in 1986.

Lord (Geoffrey) Dear was Chief Constable of the West Midlands Police from 1985 to 1990 and went on to become the Head of Her Majesty's Inspectorate of Constabulary.

Brian Dinsdale was Chief Executive at Hartlepool Council between 1988 and 2003. During his time there he oversaw the council's transition from a district to a unitary authority. He was then Chief Executive at Middlesborough Council until 2005. Since then he has pursued an active career as a consultant and as an interim manager, including five stints as interim chief executive at different local authorities.

Charles Farr was appointed Director General of the newly formed Office for Security and Counter-Terrorism (OSCT) at the Home Office in June 2007. Charles joined the Diplomatic Service in 1985 and has served at British embassies in South Africa and Jordan. He was awarded an OBE in the Queen's 2002 New Year's Honours list for his service overseas for the Foreign and Commonwealth Office and a CMG in 2009. Since 2003, he has held a number of senior posts across Whitehall concerned with security and counter-terrorism. As

Director General of OSCT, Charles is the senior official responsible for the UK counter-terrorist strategy, CONTEST.

Field Marshall the Lord (Charles) Guthrie of Craigiebank was Chief of the Defence Staff of the United Kingdom between 1997 and 2001. He also served as Chief of the General Staff, the professional head of the British Army, between 1994 and 1997. He is a cross-bench peer in the House of Lords, raised to the peerage as Baron Guthrie of Craigiebank in the City of Dundee in 2001.

Lord (Chris) Haskins was Chairman of Northern Foods from 1980 to 2002. He became the Prime Minister's 'rural tsar' at the height of the foot and mouth epidemic. He has also been Chairman of the Better Regulation Task Force and a member of the New Deal Task Force. He was a board member of Yorkshire Forward, Chairman of the Council of the Open University and Chairman of the Humber Local Enterprise Partnership.

Lord (Michael) Heseltine was a Member of Parliament in Britain from 1966 to 2001. He was a Cabinet minister in various departments from 1979 and Deputy Prime Minister from 1995 to 1997. He is founder and Chairman of the Haymarket Group, one of the largest privately owned media companies in the UK. He has written books on Europe and his political autobiography, *Life in the Jungle*.

Lord (Nigel) Lawson was Chancellor of the Exchequer between June 1983 and October 1989 and Secretary of State for Energy from September 1981 to June 1983. He is founding Chairman of the Global Warming Policy Foundation and is a past President of the British Institute of Energy Economics.

Ken Livingstone began his political career serving on Lambeth and Camden Councils before becoming Leader of the GLC in 1981 until Margaret Thatcher abolished it in 1986. He then served as Labour MP for Brent East from 1987 to 2001. Ken was elected as the newly created Mayor of London in May 2000 and was re-elected for a second term in June 2004. He has written three books: *If Voting Changed Anything They'd Abolish It* (1987), *Livingstone's Labour* (1989) and his autobiography *You Can't Say That* (2011).

Paul Martin has been Chief Executive of Wandsworth Council since 2010. He was previously Chief Executive at Sutton Council from 2005 and helped create the new unitary authority at Peterborough where he also held the post of Chief Executive.

Lord (John) Monks was General Secretary of the European Trade Union Confederation between 2003 and 2011. Prior to this he had a long career at the Trade Unions Congress where he was General Secretary between 1993 and 2003.

Sir Robert Naylor has been Chief Executive at UCLH NHS Foundation Trust since November 2000. He led the development of one of the largest building projects in the NHS to create the new world-class University College Hospital, which was handed over to the Trust in two phases from 2005. In 2009, for the second time in the last decade, the Trust achieved the status of the top-performing hospital in the NHS in the Dr Foster league tables. UCLH was designated one of the five Comprehensive Biomedical Research Centres and is a founding member of UCL Partners, an academic health science centre. He has been chairman of a number of national and regional committees and was awarded an honorary doctorate by Greenwich University in 2009.

Sir David Normington is the First Civil Service Commissioner, and the Commissioner for Public Appointments. He was Permanent Secretary at the Home Office from 2006 to 2010 and before that was Permanent Secretary at the Department for Education and Skills between 2001 and 2005.

Lord (Gus) O'Donnell was Cabinet Secretary from September 2005 to December 2011. Prior to this he was Permanent Secretary for the Treasury and Press Secretary to the Prime Minister.

Jan Parkinson is Chief Executive of the Employee Relations Institute. Before this she was Managing Director of Local Government Employers between 2006 and 2012 and Director of Human Resources at Gateshead Council between 1996 and 2006.

Sir Hayden Phillips was Permanent Secretary at the Department for Culture, Media and Sport from 1992 to 1998, and the Lord Chancellor's Department (now the Ministry of Justice) from 1998 to 2004. Prior to this he served in senior positions in the Home Office, the European Commission, the Cabinet Office and the Treasury. He has published two reports – on the 'Reform of the Honours System' in 2004, and on the 'Reform of the Funding of Political Parties' in 2007. Since leaving the civil service he has been Chairman of the National Theatre and a consultant to HRH The Prince of Wales, is a non-executive director of various companies and the independent reviewer of the adjudications of the Advertising Standards Authority.

Jonathan Powell was Tony Blair's Chief of Staff from May 1997 to June 2007. Prior to this he had a long career in the Foreign Office. Since leaving government he has held a number of positions and has now founded and runs an NGO, Inter Mediate, devoted to international conflict resolution.

James Purnell has had many senior political posts. He was Secretary of State for Work and Pensions in January 2008 until he resigned in June 2009. He was previously Secretary of State for Culture, Media and Sport, a position he took in June 2007, as part of Gordon Brown's first Cabinet. Prior to this, he was Minister of State for Pensions Reform at the Department of Work and Pensions and before becoming an MP worked as a special adviser.

Heather Rabbatts (CBE) has a singular biography ranging across law, government, sport and media. Beginning her career as a barrister at law, she then moved to become a government adviser, a senior executive in public services and the youngest CEO in the UK. During this time she began an on-screen media career as a social commentator and then moved behind the scenes: a governor of the BBC followed by an appointment as a senior executive at Channel 4 – commissioning programmes across genres and developing a range of talent development initiatives. She then became Chairman of Shed Media, a publicly listed media production and distribution company, recently bought by Time Warner. Heather is currently advising a number of UK production companies and is a non-executive for Arts Alliance (a major film/digital investment fund). She has a portfolio of non-executive roles, including Grosvenor Estates and the Royal Opera House, and she has recently been appointed to the Supervisory Board of the Foreign and Commonwealth Office and the Board of the Football Association.

John Ransford was Director of Social Services and then Acting Chief Executive at Kirklees Metropolitan Council. He moved to North Yorkshire County Council in January 1988 as Director of Social Services and served subsequently as Chief Executive from 1994 to 1999. In 1999 he joined the Local Government Association (LGA) where he was Chief Executive between 2009 and 2012.

Gill Rider was Head of the Civil Service Capability Group and Head of Profession for Civil Service HR (the top HR post in the civil service) from 2006 until 2012. Before joining the Cabinet Office, she spent 27 years at Accenture and its predecessor organizations. There, her roles included Global Chief Leadership Officer, responsible for Accenture's organization, change, HR and leadership development. She was a member of the Global Executive Committee of Accenture from 1999 to 2006. Gill has a variety of private and public sector non-executive roles, including Chair of the University of Southampton Council and President of the Chartered Institute of Personnel and Development. She was awarded an Order of the Bath (CB) in the 2011 Queen's birthday honours list.

Paul Roberts was Director of Education in Nottingham and subsequently in Haringey, leading the government intervention in Haringey Council. He was a director of Capita Strategic Education Services before joining the Improvement and Development Agency

(IDeA) for local government. At IDeA he was Director of Strategy and subsequently Managing Director, overseeing the organization's £50m programmes of work based on knowledge management, peer review and support for local authority elected members. As author of the joint DfES/DCMS report 'Nurturing Creativity in Young People', Paul was adviser to government ministers on the development of the cultural offer for young people and is now Chair of the Trustees for Creativity, Culture and Education (**www.cceengland.org**) as well as holding board positions with Mountview Academy of Theatre Arts, Nottingham Contemporary, the Greenwood Academies Trust, the Innovation Unit and the Public Services Innovation Laboratory Committee at the National Endowment for Science, Technology and the Arts (NESTA). Paul is an FRSA and was awarded an OBE in 2008 for services to education and the creative industries.

Sir Peter Rogers was an adviser to Boris Johnson on regeneration, growth and enterprise from 2011 to 2012, Chief Executive of the London Development Agency between 2008 and 2011 and Chief Executive of the City of Westminster between 1999 and 2008. Before that he was involved with the transport industry for 15 years.

Stephen Taylor has been a business adviser for 30 years. Stephen has worked with the board of every government department, the NHS, the Bank of England and most large government agencies. In the private sector he has worked similarly with a dozen FTSE companies, including Boots, Philips, Thames Water, Esso, W H Smith, Balfour Beatty and British Airways. A feature in *The Independent* described him as 'the most sought after consultant in the UK' and a *Times* leader as 'a ubiquitous figure in Whitehall'.

Lord (Andrew) Turnbull was Cabinet Secretary from September 2002 to September 2005. Prior to that he had several senior government roles, including Permanent Secretary to the Treasury and Principal Private Secretary to the Prime Minister.

Sir Robin Wales is the directly elected Mayor of Newham. He has been part of local government since 1982 and served as a councillor from 1982 to 1986 and from 1992 until becoming leader of Newham Council in 1995. In 2002 he won the election to be the borough's first ever directly elected mayor and was subsequently re-elected in 2006 and 2010. In 2006 he was appointed by the Secretary of State to sit on the board of the London Organizing Committee for the Olympic Games (LOCOG).

Nick Walkley is Chief Executive of the London Borough of Haringey. Prior to this he was Chief Executive at the London Borough of Barnet and has had a number of senior roles in central and local government.

Ian Watmore was Permanent Secretary in the Cabinet Office, working also as the government's Chief Operating Officer overseeing the government's efficiency and reform agenda. He had rejoined the civil service after a year as Chief Executive of the Football Association. Prior to this, he was Permanent Secretary of the department now known as Business Innovation and Skills, he was in Number 10 where he worked directly for Tony Blair as the Head of the Prime Minister's Delivery Unit, and in the Cabinet Office as the government's Chief Information Officer. He joined the civil service after a 24-year business career in IT and consulting, culminating as Accenture's UK Managing Director from 2000 to 2004, and President of the Management Consultants Association in 2003. He is Chair of the Migraine Trust and non-executive director to two sports bodies, the English Institute for Sport, which provides sports science and medicine services to Olympic athletes, and ER2015, the organization charged with staging the Rugby Union World Cup in 2015.

Lord (Richard) Wilson was Cabinet Secretary between 1998 and 2002. He held many senior posts in the civil service, including Permanent Secretary at the Department of the Environment and Permanent Under-Secretary at the Home Office. He was Master of Emmanuel College, Cambridge from 2002 until 2012.

INDEX